AQUATICS
FOR
SPECIAL
POPULATIONS

F

YMCA of the USA

Library of Congress Cataloging-in-Publication Data

Aquatics for special populations.

Bibliography: p.
1. Aquatic exercises—Therapeutic use.
2. Physically handicapped—Rehabilitation.
I. YMCA of the USA.
RM727.H8A68   1987   615.8'2   86-28288
ISBN 0-87322-097-8 (Human Kinetics)

Cover Design and Layout: Jack Davis

Copyright © 1987 YMCA of the USA
Published for the YMCA of the USA by Human Kinetics Publishers, Inc.

ISBN: 0-87322-097-8

Printed in the United States of America

10 9 8 7 6 5 4 3 2 1

Copies of this book may be purchased from the YMCA Program Store, Box 5077, Champaign, IL 61820, (217) 351-5077.

Contents

Preface

The YMCA of the USA has been a national leader and pioneer in programming for special populations since the early 1950s. Aquatics programs for special populations have gained acceptance and popularity both locally and globally, and have helped each participant to live up to his or her full human potential.

Special populations include individuals with physical, mental, emotional, or social disabilities. Program participants often have a number of disabilities. More importantly, each program participant has a wide range of *abilities*. In YMCA aquatic programs we concentrate on these abilities.

A person's disabilities may require only minor accommodations. The disabled person can surmount physical or intellectual problems much more readily than the psychological and emotional barriers that other people sometimes create. At the YMCA we work with persons of all ethnic groups, ages, economic levels, and abilities. We strive to overcome barriers through empathy and understanding, and we concentrate on similarities rather than differences among all people. We work to develop the mind, body, and spirit of our members—the disabled and the able-bodied—through programs such as aquatics. We believe every person in an aquatics class should relax, have fun, and succeed. Success in aquatics can begin a cycle of success even for those who have previously experienced many failures. One small triumph builds on another, bringing confidence and hope.

YMCA aquatics for the disabled began at the grass roots level. The first regional YMCA aquatics manual for special populations was published in 1960 by the Longview, Washington, YMCA. Grace Demmery Reynolds and Esther M. Dedrick edited that manual for the Pacific Northwest Area Council Meeting of YMCAs in Spokane. Since then thousands of people with special needs have benefited from aquatics programs provided by the YMCA alone and in collaboration with other agencies. In 1973, the first national manual of aquatics for the disabled, *A Swimming Program for the Handicapped*, was published. From 1973 to 1982 the YMCA directed several projects of the Bureau of Education for the Handicapped, Office of Special Education and Rehabilitative Services: Project Aquatics from 1973 to 1976; Project Aquatics Mainstreaming (Project PAM) from 1976 to 1979; and Project Mainstreaming Activities for Youth (Project MAY) from 1979 to 1982. Foundations, agencies, and individuals have contributed substantially; all projects have involved the significant cooperation of numerous agencies.

YMCAs throughout the world currently offer aquatics and other programs for special populations. This manual is a special resource for you, the instructor and program developer committed to providing aquatics for individuals whose disabilities may require adaptive approaches and techniques. Your training has provided you with the background to operate a good aquatics program. This manual can help you to adapt what you already know to meet the needs of special populations. If you are a newcomer to special populations, the information and references in this manual will help you in developing a quality program. If you are experienced in this area, it may serve as a review. Select freely from the material dealing with your special areas of interest or need. Aquatics programs and resourceful, talented instructors can provide an excellent avenue for developing the total person.

Acknowledgments

Our thanks to the following people for their time, interest, and efforts:

Grace D. Reynolds
Office of Special Populations, YMCA of the USA

Dallas S. Dedrick
National Council of YMCAs (past member)

Esther M. Dedrick, Consultant

Mary B. Essert, Consultant

Henry Goodwin, Consultant

Syma R. Jelen, Writer

Daryl D. Jenkins, Consultant

Marjorie M. Murphy, Associate Director
Program Services, YMCA of the USA

The following staff of the YMCA of the USA, Office of Special Populations, assisted:

Mary V. Dudley, Program Assistant

M. June Schaff, Administrative Assistant

The following partial list of names identifies people who have shared information with us or have sent material:

Ruth Alexander
Department of Physical Education for Women
University of Florida

Lloyd C. Arnold, Former Director
Health and Physical Education
National Board of YMCAs

Donald J. Cawrse, Executive Director
Regional Family YMCA
Framingham, Massachusetts

James Hollis
West Chester University, Pennsylvania

Joan E. Lee
Vocational and Rehabilitation Institute
Calgary, Alberta, Canada

Col. William P. McCahill, USMC (retired)
Arlington, Virginia

Alexander Melleby
New York City YMCA

Robert Orozco, Former Director of Aquatics
National Board of YMCAs

Jennifer Port, PhD
Regional Education Service Agency
Parkersburg, West Virginia

James Scanlon
Temple University
Philadelphia, Pennsylvania

John Schiebel
Naples YMCA
Naples, Florida

John C. Sevier
Springfield, Pennsylvania

Deborah Sheffrin
Rehabilitation Institute
Chicago, Illinois

Julian U. Stein
George Mason University
Fairfax, Virginia

Robert E. Sweet
Dutchess County YMCA
Poughkeepsie, New York

M.J. Tash, Consultant
Dutchess County YMCA
Poughkeepsie, New York

Kathleen Wilson
Whittier YMCA
Whittier, California

Introduction

Much has been written about the need for special programs to serve people with disabilities. Until recently disabled persons were almost always segregated into their own programs. As our understanding of disabilities increased, an awareness grew that such restricted settings may not provide the best service to the disabled population. Major changes in attitudes, values, and laws have contributed to new approaches.

The "mainstreamed" or integrated aquatics program includes persons with disabilities in general aquatics activities. Many consider mainstreaming to be an effective and popular programming method. When mainstreaming is based on the idealistic view that mixing disabled and able-bodied populations is always positive, however, both program leaders and participants may be disappointed.

Mainstreaming is a continuum. At one extreme, a totally segregated program serves a narrowly defined special population. At the other extreme, a totally integrated program serves all individuals whether or not they have special needs. The totally segregated program may be part of a mainstreaming continuum if it is designed to lead to a participant's inclusion in a less segregated program. Effective programs with various degrees of integration can be created to meet the specific needs of individual class members. Some participants may benefit most from segregated classes.

The term *special population* may loosely be defined as any group of people with more than normal needs. People may become part of a special needs group as the result of illness, accident, or temporary or permanent loss or impairment of some part of their ability to function. Special populations include people of all ages, both sexes, and every ethnic group. Any group that requires extra help to establish a common basis of interaction in life is a special population.

Aquatics is a particularly attractive activity for special populations. Water is a great equalizer; it often minimizes disabilities. Everyone can experience success in aquatics with the guidance and understanding of a good instructor.

Developing information about the needs of the individuals to be served is the essence of an effective aquatics program. If program development efforts are beginning without a defined special population in mind, a need statement will help in selecting a small group from the larger population. Then the ability and resources for meeting the needs of this specific group can be realistically evaluated. If a program will be serving a preselected group at the request of the community, the need statement can help in clarifying program objectives; the instructor can identify the group's need more clearly and communicate more effectively.

The need statement is most effective when it is a concise description. It should cover the number of individuals in the defined population to be served, the types and number of disabilities, potential leadership, specific requirements for programming, community resources, sources of funding, and support services that will be required, such as transportation.

In this manual we offer practical advice on developing aquatics programming for special populations.

- In chapter 1 we review the educational, recreational, and other values of aquatics.
- In chapter 2 we review planning, public relations, and program implementation.
- In chapter 3 we offer teaching approaches and techniques.
- In chapter 4 we provide health and safety recommendations.
- In chapter 5 we detail leadership requirements and guidelines.
- In chapter 6 we discuss facilities and equipment.
- In chapter 7 we describe various disabilities.
- In chapter 8 we outline YMCA certification institutes and training.

A glossary of terms is provided in the back of this manual. References to other resources are included in appendices A, B, and C and should be used to help expand knowledge and approach.

Why Aquatics? 1

Historically, activities involving water have been used to decrease stress and facilitate physical and emotional rehabilitation. The famous Roman baths were originally constructed for the use of battle-weary Roman soldiers. Swimming and water exercise were used routinely for rehabilitating the wounded during and after World War II. In recent years, recreational, instructional, competitive, and prescribed swimming activities have increased significantly for persons of all ages and with all types of disabilities.

Swimming is a logical, effective, and supportable community program for improving the acceptance, self-esteem, and physical and mental health of disabled individuals. Aquatics programs for those with disabilities have several advantages.

- Swimming and other aquatics activities have become so popular that many communities now have appropriate facilities. Opportunities for training qualified leaders also are readily available. Upgrading instructional skills and modifying existing facilities can be done in practical, cost-effective ways.

- Regardless of the nature or severity of the disability, an appropriate water activity usually can be found. Aquatics covers a wide range of activities from shallow water wading to competitive racing, synchronized diving, and underwater sports. Water exercise, sports, games, and therapeutic water activities are available to people with widely varying skill levels. With proper training—perhaps in a pool at first—and with adequate equipment and suitable attire, including Personal Flotation Devices (PFDs) that have United States Coast Guard approval, many people with disabilities can participate in canoeing, boating, kayaking, waterskiing, and other water activities.

- Water provides buoyancy. Gravitational forces are reduced substantially in water so that parts of the body can be moved with less muscular effort. Muscle tone and coordination can be improved, and differences among individuals are less apparent.

- Aquatics programs can enhance participants' self-esteem. Accomplishing even the simplest skill can bring a measure of success. For people with disabilities, the most important accomplishment in the world may be to walk alone for the first time—in the water.

- Aquatics develops physical fitness, strength, endurance, flexibility, balance, and mobility. This may improve mental and emotional health as well as physical health.

- Aquatics provides an excellent opportunity for personal adjustment. Participants learn to relate to others in an acceptable manner. School, club, and community activities as well as other special events are open to those in aquatics programs. These activities help to improve social consciousness, establish friendships, and prepare participants for greater involvement in the community.

- Water activities help to improve perception and vocabulary. Participants in aquatics programs also learn to identify colors, shapes, sizes, and the words associated with various activities.

- Water activities are democratic. They focus on ability rather than disability and emphasize mutual acceptance and inclusion.

- Water activities are fun.

Aquatics programs can promote physical fitness and well-being for disabled people of all ages. Such programs need no special equipment—although some equipment such as hoops and colorful weights may be fun—and can be set up even in limited areas of water. Water exercise is good for muscle tone, flexibility, posture, breathing, endurance, range of motion, release of stress, and overall fitness.

In the following chapters we offer tested suggestions, based on years of practical experience, for initiating and conducting successful aquatics programs.

Providing Programs for Special Populations

2

Your organization has chosen to develop an aquatics program for a special population—now you need to lay the groundwork with thorough planning and make the program a reality.

Planning Your Program

Aquatics programs for special populations succeed because of detailed planning by many segments of the community. Planning includes careful evaluation of the suitability, accessibility, availability, and safety of facilities; the availability of trained supervisory and support personnel; transportation; public relations; and, of course, financing. When possible, programs should be planned with the input of current and potential program participants.

Any aquatics program for special populations must be tailored to the number of participants and to the nature and severity of their disabilities. Programs should be evaluated for their mainstreaming potential.

Schools, health agencies, child-find programs, recreational departments, and special interest groups are good resources for contacting the disabled and learning about needs within the community. Print and electronic media such as newspapers, magazines, church bulletins, radio, and television can be used to identify disabled persons who are not involved with other community programs. Personal contact with potential participants, parents, and guardians as well as professionals can generate and sustain interest in a program.

Preliminary Planning

Essential components of a successful aquatics program for special populations include broad-based community awareness, cooperation, adapted facilities, careful supervision, trained personnel, and special understanding and empathy among all associated personnel. With these components in place, many conventional aquatics programs can be adapted for the disabled.

A sponsoring group comprised of a broad spectrum of community representatives with an interest in special populations, program participants, and their families can greatly facilitate planning for aquatics programs. This group can serve as a program initiator and catalyst. Subcommittees within the sponsoring group or individual members with special expertise can take responsibility for financing, public relations, recordkeeping, program content, evaluation, recruitment, and leadership training. The YMCA, because of its philosophy and tradition, is an excellent sponsoring organization. Communities without Ys can recruit interested agencies as sponsors. Other community members who can be asked to join the committee include interested consumers, family members, physicians, and allied health personnel such as social workers, therapeutic recreation specialists, educators, and therapists.

Transportation

Adequate, practical transportation can mean the difference between a program's success and failure. Local transportation authorities and private businesses in the area may be able to assist with transportation. Schools may have specially equipped buses or vans. Dial-a-Van, Care-a-Van, the local Retired Senior Volunteer Program, service clubs, and even taxicab companies may be able to help with special arrangements. Many YMCAs already own vehicles for program use that can be adapted or have arrangements with nursing homes whose vans are equipped to accommodate wheelchairs. Specially trained drivers are essential to successfully transporting disabled people who require assistance.

Funding

Aquatics programs for special populations should not be any more expensive than other aquatics programs. While many disabled people can be mainstreamed, facility adaptations and additional trained personnel should be considered when budgeting for aquatics programs for those with disabilities. Only when adequate funding is available and a realistic budget has been approved should aquatics programs for special populations be implemented. The following should be considered when financing a new program:

- Staff costs depend on the number of staff members needed, including the number of volunteers available.
- Pool costs are contingent on individual pool expenses.
- Equipment costs can be minimized by innovative use of material. Lifts and transfer equipment may be needed.
- Marketing and promotional costs will be small if public service news media are used. All promotional material should be of professional quality. Use YMCA brochures and other resources (see next section, "Public Relations").

Funding may be obtained from a variety of sources. Program service and membership fees can provide some funds. Scholarships, individual donations, bequests, memorials, and group donations will be forthcoming if program committee members, the YMCA, or professional fundraisers lay the proper groundwork and follow up on potential funding sources on a regular basis. City, county, and state funds, school funds, federal funding, and funding from private foundations should be investigated and appropriate applications made. Occasionally organizations already working with special needs groups will share their facilities; this can prove to be cost effective. In addition, allowing other groups to use YMCA facilities in exchange for resources or at a fee can provide further funding.

Many participants can pay their own fees and assist in supporting the program. Fees for service and educational allotments may provide funding. Third party payments such as labor and industries, Medicaid, Medicare, Social Security, and insurance company payments underwrite some costs. The state agency handling workers' compensation should be approached by an appropriate volunteer or staff person for industrial injury claims.

Organizations or individuals may establish scholarships for disabled program participants when they are told a need exists. A good rule is to ask for what you need. Grants may be given by matching funds already raised by the community. Such funds may be awarded dollar for dollar or in other ways. Check with local government sources and private foundations in your area about grants available. United Way allocations, revenue sharing funds, vendor contributions, and outright purchase of services are additional sources of funding.

Public Relations *

Public relations is one way to build the reputation of an aquatics program and sell it to the public. A good promotion plan can communicate that the program is excellent, comprehensive, and open at reasonable cost to the community. Appropriate publicity can convey credibility to the target audience of disabled people and their families. A local YMCA can plan a public relations program the same way it plans any good program—by setting goals, analyzing the target audience, determining the message, and devising strategies to reach this audience.

To set goals first decide how big the program should be. How many participants will ideally enroll in the first session? How many community people should be aware of the program? How many others—health care professionals, educators, business people—should be reached? The larger the goals, the more will need to be done to reach them.

Analyzing the public requires defining the targeted audience. The audience undoubtedly will be disabled people and their

*This section from *Arthritis Foundation YMCA Aquatic Program: Guidelines and Procedures* (pp. 14-17) by YMCA of the USA and the Arthritis Foundation, 1985, Champaign, IL: Human Kinetics. Copyright 1985 by YMCA of the USA and the Arthritis Foundation. Adapted by permission.

families who are interested in aquatics for recreational, therapeutic, and social purposes. Fitness, wellness, swimming, and the YMCA holistic philosophy (mind, body, and spirit) may be a significant part of a disabled person's decision to enroll in a Y program. In analyzing the public, identify the kinds of places the targeted participants or potential participants now frequent. Which schools do they attend? What about churches or retirement homes? What kinds of newspapers and periodicals do they read? What radio and TV stations do they listen to?

The basic message should be that the YMCA is conducting a high-quality aquatics program. The program should be clearly explained, along with who is conducting classes, what the classes consist of, when they will be held, and why people should join. Explain how to enroll and provide a phone number to call and an address to visit for more information.

Selecting publicity strategies entails defining the specific promotional techniques needed. The secret is simply to get the program's name and message in the periodicals that the targeted audience reads, in the shows they listen to, and in the places they go.

Techniques for conveying the message are not complex. Regardless of who the target public is, print and broadcast publicity most likely will reach them. Free publicity, including stories on radio and TV and in newspapers and magazines, should be the goal, not paid advertisements. Obtaining free media coverage is not impossible. Not-for-profit organizations are good information sources, and journalists always are looking for information.

Types of coverage vary with the way the story is presented. Whether on radio or TV, in the local weekly or the city daily, journalists have three basic ways to present a story:

- *News stories* concentrate on the "hard facts" about changes, developments, and events that have just occurred or will happen soon. The news usually occupies the front pages of a periodical and the morning, noon, and evening broadcasts. A news story could be an announcement about the new, comprehensive aquatics for the disabled program offered by the Y.

- *Feature stories* give the background behind a news event or of people in the news. They are often called "human interest stories." A feature could be a profile of a person enrolled in the program; a radio panel discussion about swimming for the disabled; a "how-to" article on sports,

safety, and rescue for special populations; or a TV inter-
view with an aquatics leader, health care specialist, or
educator.

- *Editorials* are opinion pieces written by journalists, editors,
and qualified experts. To give the public the opportunity
to express an opinion, most newspapers have "Letters to
the Editor" sections. Radio and TV have "rebuttal" spots
on their new shows. Editors and progam directors may
be convinced to run an editorial authored by the YMCA
or someone in their organization about the benefits of
aquatics for the disabled.

To obtain media coverage an organization must get to the
people who can publicize its cause—editors, reporters, and program directors. Media people may seem intimidating, but there's
no need to be shy. They have a job to do—providing information
to the public—and the availability of aquatics programs for special populations is valuable information that others will want to
hear. The following "do's and don'ts" should help make media
contact easier:

- *Do* study the local media. Listen to the shows and read the
periodicals to determine exactly which reporters and editors cover what specific topics. Remember, there may be
more than one editor or reporter at a medium outlet who
should be contacted, such as the feature and the news
editor at the local paper.
- *Do* cultivate a relationship with the media. Call or visit to
ask if journalists are on deadline and arrange to meet them
at their office, at the YMCA, or at a local restaurant.
- *Don't* expect instant publicity from a first meeting. The goal
is simply to become familiar with the media, to tell them
about the program, and to ask how and when they like to
be informed about coming events and story ideas.
- *Do* maintain a relationship with contacts. Call them with
interesting items. Hand deliver press releases when possible. Talk with them about story and photo ideas and in-
vite them to classes or events. Personal contact increases
the chance of getting coverage.
- *Do* send out press releases of all newsworthy events. Every
time a new class starts, a class "graduates," or a special
event is planned, that's *news*. Writing a press release is not
difficult, but it demands simplicity. Be clean, clear, and
concise. Stick to the facts—the who, what, when, where,

why, and how of the story. Most news stories are written with the most important facts first and the least important last.

- *Don't* forget to consider all angles of a story. Aside from news, offer the media good feature or human interest ideas, such as a profile of a former participant who is now an instructor or a photograph of a Special Olympics winner from a Y class.

- *Don't* harass the media by constantly calling to see if they will run a story and don't pressure them with references to any advertising the YMCA buys from them.

- *Do* follow up on press releases that have been sent to verify if they were received, if the press found them helpful, and if the reporter needs any further information.

- *Don't* forget to contact all local media and all the different reporters and editors at each outlet. Keep a list of everyone contacted and their interest in a story.

Aside from news and feature stories in the media, many other techniques are available for publicizing aquatics for special populations.

Public service announcements (PSAs). Most radio and TV stations devote a small portion of their air time to broadcasting announcements that inform the public about helpful goods and services or ask for support and donations. Not-for-profit groups should have no problem obtaining this kind of publicity. Stations may want a script or tape, often in 10-, 30-, or 60-second spots. Call or write the station's public service director and ask about the station's requirements for PSAs.

Speakers bureau. Speaking to community organizations is an effective way to communicate a message. Ask the local Chamber of Commerce for lists of community groups, then contact these groups to see if they are interested in speakers. Don't neglect the obvious groups such as PTAs, church sisterhoods, men's clubs, and senior citizen organizations. Even if an appearance is only for 5 minutes, it will have a strong impact. Slides and audiovisual aids can enhance a presentation, but they are not a requirement.

Literature. Brochures, posters, newsletters, and direct mail pieces are all important in spreading program awareness. When writing promotional literature, think of the audience to be reached. Keep the message simple and don't overload the copy with too many words. Avoid jargon and use plain, eye-catching graphics to attract attention. A brochure or handout should be accompanied by detailed information about dates, times, places, and procedures for registering for classes.

Letters. A brochure, handout, or letter of information should be mailed promptly following any telephone inquiry.

Special events. Meetings, conferences, open houses, exhibits, and displays are great ways to reach the public directly and to gain media coverage. Be imaginative. Not only can the Y sponsor its own exhibit, it can set up a booth at another group's open house.

Advertising. Advertising is usually paid publicity. Some newspapers do offer free classified ads, and these should be taken advantage of. The impact of advertising is strong, but much of it depends on the frequency and timing of the ads. Consult the advertising representatives of local media for help in planning an advertising schedule that will effectively communicate the message.

Word of mouth. Experience with similar programs has demonstrated over and over that the word-of-mouth method is by far the best for producing new enrollees.

Class observation. Potential participants should be able to observe a class in action.

Community calendars. Many newspapers, radio stations, and TV stations have a calendar of coming events in the community. Announcements of registration dates and special events should appear in this calendar.

Photographs. When it comes to publicity, a picture is worth more than multitudes of words. Most people pay more attention to the photographs in a newspaper than to the copy. However, photos are most effective when well done, so hire a competent photographer to take publicity shots. (Many local newspapers will send one to shoot pictures on site.) Be sure also to obtain permission from participants or their guardians to use their photographs and names.

Implementing Your Program

Some participants with disabilities require no adaptations in facilities or programs. For others, special programs can be designed to meet individual needs. The disabilities may be small or great, due to a single cause or to multiple causes. Disabilities can affect one or many parts of the body. Yet most aquatic skills can be mastered by most people. Every participant will master skills in a different way, depending on ability and how well accommodations can be made. Ability and determination are keys to mastering water skills.

With patience and understanding, instructors can guide and assist participants in achieving success. Innovative instructors can help participants learn in their own way and at their own speed. When one approach does not work, other approaches and adaptations can be found. Each person's needs must be considered individually, even in group instruction.

Program Sessions

Sessions may be designed for various purposes. Some of the most common are the following:

Therapy sessions. These sessions must be under the leadership of a licensed registered therapist, who should work under a physician's direction. The individual program prescription should be developed through a team approach. With the consent of appropriate medical personnel, thereapy program participants also can engage in fitness, instructional, and recreational water programs.

Another type of therapy session can have socialization as its goal. Participants may be referred by mental health agencies, health and human resource departments, physicians, drug and alcohol centers, or other places. Therapeutic recreational programs should be planned, implemented, and evaluated regularly by a leadership team. (See chapter 5 for more on leadership teams.)

Orientation programs. These programs should be offered to everyone entering aquatics activities at least once. They should include an introduction to transportation services, the parking area, the general building, the locker rooms, the showers, and the pool area. Potential participants should have an opportunity to observe a class in session. Family members should be encouraged to attend orientation.

Instructional programs. These are programs that assist people in acquiring the skills needed to feel comfortable in and to move through the water. Adaptations of the skills taught in progressive swim programs may be made.

Recreation programs. Such programs have become increasingly popular over the past 20 years for people with disabilities. Aquatics recreation programs are ideal for participants who want to exercise, socialize, and relax. As a safety measure, programmers for regular and special programs must keep in mind that those participating in aquatic recreation or leisure programs may not mention that they have any specific conditions or disabilities or are taking medications. Some participants may be substance abusers; alcohol is responsible for the majority of aquatic accidents.

Fitness/exercise programs. These programs involve those with disabilities in mainstream as well as separate activities. Manuals on water exercise and aquatics for the arthritic are available at the YMCA Program Store (see appendix A, Bibliography).

Water exercise. Such exercise can help participants feel and look better. Water exercise is an ideal way to improve muscle tone, flexibility, and posture. It increases endurance and range of motion, helps manage weight, releases stress, and develops cardiovascular fitness.

Guidelines for Class Activity

To ensure the participants' safety, a physician's permission should be obtained for any person with a disability beginning an exercise program. Participants' therapists and physicians should be involved in planning aquatics activities. A lifeguard must be on deck while the instructor is leading exercises. Participants should be watched carefully, and exercise programs should be tailored for individuals' needs and skills. Experts say that water activity can be adjusted from near zero output to maximum output; the instructor can help each person monitor individual expenditure of energy and recognize his or her unique rhythm and comfort zone.

Warmups should include adjustment to the water and simple stretching followed, when possible, by walking or light jogging in chest- or shoulder-deep water. Back injuries require special care. Participants should assume a bent-knee or rounded, fetal-like position for exercise. Stretching, when done regularly in a relaxed manner, reduces muscular tension and thus promotes freedom of movement. Warmups should be done in a head-to-foot progression, using regular, deep breathing. Bouncing and dynamic motion are not as safe as continuous slight movement of the feet and legs. Cross steps or bent long steps to the front or sides are safer than straight leg lifts or backward walking, which may stress the knees. In knees-up exercises, holding the hands beneath the thighs relieves pressure.

Muscular flexibility, strength, and endurance exercises should be performed according to the following guidelines:

- Work one muscle group or similar muscle groups at the same time, such as both arms and legs.
- Work each muscle group for both strength and flexibility.
- Work at least two exercises per muscle group.
- Alternate between opposing muscle groups.

The correct amount of exercise varies for each person. Students can evaluate on a scale of 1 to 10 how they feel about the energy they have expended and their level of fatigue. Most people know their body's rhythm and comfort zone. If something hurts, they should stop.

A rigorous exercise program may need to be modified for some individuals. Signs to watch for include undue fatigue during exercise; difficulty in breathing; dizziness; loss of normal coordination; tightness in the chest; clenched teeth; arm, jaw, ear, or upper back pain; irregular heart rate after exercise; and aggravation of musculoskeletal problems. If fatigue, discomfort, or pain occur, stop the exercises. Consult with the participant's physician and team members for their recommendations.

For those with special needs, aerobic (cardiovascular) fitness can provide these benefits:

- Lower blood pressure
- Lower triglyceride levels
- Lower heart rate at rest and during exercise
- Increased endurance
- Increased lean body tissue

For maximum benefit, workouts depend on intensity, frequency, and duration. Workouts should be done with enough intensity to keep the pulse in the target zone for 20 minutes. Exercise should be done for a minimum of 3 nonconsecutive days a week in chest- or shoulder-deep water; it should be preceded by a 20-minute warmup and followed by a cool-down period. Workouts should increase in intensity and duration progressively.

Determining resting heart rate is simple: Take the pulse early in the morning for several mornings, and calculate the average number of beats per minute. Then multiply the number of beats by 6. The American Heart Association recommends the following way to determine exercise heart rate: Subtract the person's age from 220. Multiply the answer by .60 to get the number of beats per minute for minimum exercise heart rate (EHR). Then multiply by .80 to get maximum exercise heart rate. The target lies between the minimum and maximum heart rates. Participants with specific conditions should work within the EHRs recommended by their physicians. Swimmers' EHRs are lower than those of joggers.

Heart rate is elevated when large muscle groups are vigorously exercised. Once a routine has been established, exercises should be gradually increased to maintain target heart rate. When possible, students should monitor heart rate four times per session. This number includes a beginning and ending (or recovery) heart rate.

Music—informal singing, tapes, or records—and equipment can add to the effectiveness and fun of exercise. Equipment can include flotation devices, weights, wands, surgical tubing, water-resistant cuffs, kickboards, balls, and hula hoops. Creativity, innovation, and flexibility are also important when working with disabled students. Some may join regular fitness programs (aquaerobics at the YMCA is probably most rigorous, while arthritis aquatics is gentlest); others may want to work out only in classes specificially for those with special conditions.

Maintain a moderate pace; watch for signs of overexertion; discourage competiton among class members; maintain a friendly, fun atmosphere; and adjust workouts for daily and seasonal differences in temperature and humidity. Follow these guidelines to create a worthwhile exercise program.

Teaching Special *3* Populations

Experienced instructors stress that concentrating on abilities, not disabilities, is essential in working with all populations. Regular teaching techniques and progressions can be used with those who have disabilities. Adjustments and innovations can be made on an individual basis. Begin with skills the student can successfully perform, then gradually introduce other skills based on personal ability. If questions arise about individuals, such as how best to work with them, how much activity they are permitted, or what their limitations are, first talk with the participants, then consult a physician or other member of the health care team if necessary.

Experience shows that a structured program preceded or followed by free swim time works well. When appropriate, exercises and skills should be tried on land as well as in water. Many instructors can work with individuals with a variety of disabilities in the same class.

Have a working knowledge of wheelchairs and prosthetic devices before classes begin. Practice pushing, locking, and lifting wheelchairs and consult each individual about the care of any prosthetic device. Experience in lifting and transferring individuals is very important. (See orthopedic disabilities in chapter 7 and lifts and transfers in chapter 4.)

Approaches to Teaching

Some teachers work best in a structured program, while others prefer more flexibility. No single approach or teaching sequence will guarantee success for every instructor with every student. New and original approaches in teaching are needed. When working with severely disabled people, more than one instructor or an instructor and assistant may be necessary. Most physical activities require a minimal level of strength, endurance, agility, balance, power, speed, flexibility, and coordination.

To teach new skills, break them down into sequential progressions that include periods of warm-up routine, repetition, relaxation, and cooldown. Skills should be explained in simple terms, clarified in two or three different ways, demonstrated, and practiced. The skills acquired in an aquatics program may well transfer to learning and social development in other areas.

A good teacher should be able to motivate the student. A daily evaluation sheet for recording achievement, kept in a folder for the swimmer, can be an invaluable aid. This evaluation, along with background information and skill sheets, is an important part of the student's general education record. Most agencies today have computers, which are ideal for updating and accessing records. (See appendix B, Forms and Lists for Instructors, for sample recordkeeping forms.)

The success of a swimming lesson may depend on how the instructor interacts with students. Discipline must be maintained both in and out of the water. Be empathetic, not sympathetic, when dealing with students. Reinforcement is also important. A smile or verbal encouragement, extra free time for a job well done, and awards at the end of a session work well as reinforcers, especially with children.

Games and toys provide an opportunity for learning skills through fun. Well-supervised competitive games can help stimulate interest and give students a much needed sense of accomplishment. Synchronized swimming, water safety, lifesaving, and the use of music all help make the aquatic program interesting and enjoyable. Some participants and instructors may wish to use flotation equipment to assist with movement and activity. Movement exploration encourages the student to gain independence and body awareness.

Circuit training and interval training make the learning process much more interesting. Circuit training enables a student to move among different stations and progress at an individual pace based on his or her own level of fitness and skill; interval training enables the student to progress at his or her own rate, by performing a series of activities at his or her own level or pace for a specified length of time. Circuit training and interval training often are combined to provide for maximum student participation. Students remain at each station for a specified length of time—10 seconds, 30 seconds, 1 minute. In this way everyone moves from station to station at the same time, reducing confusion, eliminating waiting in line at certain stations, and minimizing unnecessary movement. As students improve in ability and fitness, the time spent at each station can be increased gradually. When practical, an instructor or aide should be at each station to provide greater individual attention for every student.

Movement Exploration in the Water

Movement exploration is an effective, enjoyable way of reaching out to a student. All skills planned for a class should be organized as problem-solving situations. The student should be given freedom to explore and solve problems in a manner unique to his or her individual ability, thus learning the movements needed to perform a particular skill and how to control these movements.

By exploring creatively, instructors and students can learn to use asymmetrical and symmetrical movements in the water. Students can try innovative ways to employ these movements with the guidance of their instructors. Some examples of movement exploration activities are as follows:

- *Adjustment to the water*—feeling, splashing, kicking, walking, blowing bubbles, jumping, pushing, and pulling
- *Breath control*—blowing through a straw or pipe; blowing a Ping-Pong ball; blowing water held in the hands; retrieving objects such as washcloths, sponges, and weighted toys; touching the feet with the hands; blowing bubbles across the pool; and blowing bubbles under the water
- *Movement in the water*—feeling body parts; moving individual body parts; balancing with the help of the instructor or a partner; sitting on the bottom of the pool; running, leaping, and galloping in the water; skipping and sliding;

throwing, catching, and kicking in the water; and experimenting with ways to move from one side of the pool to the other, from one point to another, or from one line or slope to another

- *Exploration of positions in the water*—while holding onto the side with a partner or alone; while standing in the water with a partner or alone; while moving in different directions (forward, sideways, backward, in reverse, to the left or right); and while moving in circles, straight lines, or other geometrical patterns
- *Space and body awareness*—using a towel, hula hoop, or other object, stepping over or under the object, jumping over it, or ducking under it; using imagination or plastic boxes, exploring such concepts as in, out, around, or through
- *Locomotion*—with assistive devices such as kickboards or barbells, moving slowly or quickly; practicing and timing movements; and testing endurance

Movement education can be taught directly, giving details of moving forward in the water; indirectly, exploring ways of getting from one side of the pool to the other; and by setting limitations, finding a way of getting from one side of the pool to the other, using only the arms, the legs, one arm, or one leg.

Tell students to move in their personal space by stretching, curling, twisting, and shaking. Then have them move without actual locomotion—they can rattle a toy or shoot a rubber band. Another time have the students move within their personal space first with the accompaniment of balls and next by adding words to describe movements. Then use balls to further illustrate *under, over,* and *through.*

Later have students move in the general space in various directions and on different levels. Rolling and crawling are ways of moving. Using rhythm instruments, such as a drum with a fuzzy cover, and adding balls for movement in different directions and levels can be fun. Objects can be used in the water on different levels. Students can travel through different paths, swimming on the water, under the water, bobbing over the water, and diving for objects at the bottom of the pool.

Help students become aware of their bodies, asking "What can you move?" Let them find body parts that bend, stretch, circle, and change. Students can touch body parts to each other, then move those parts as far as possible from each other. Working with partners in various ways, students can make a bridge to go around and through; play follow the leader, creating a rhythm pattern to follow; and achieve balance with partners. Partners can choreograph a movement sequence in the water showing changes of speed, level, and direction. These movements can lead to synchronized swimming.

Allow students to move about in the water without being compelled to swim. Swimming is a goal toward which student and teacher work, but that goal may be reached in many ways. Beginners should not be rushed; they should first be allowed to gain reasonable security in the water. Efforts should be directed at developing basic safety survival skills at all times.

Working with those who have disabilities is often more challenging and rewarding than working with other segments of the population. Each success develops confidence and skills on which to build.

Listening and understanding are essential to teaching. Program participants often can explain how a skill can be adapted to their use. Listening attentively and seriously and allowing time for explanations ultimately will save much time and frustration.

Occasionally you may find working with a particular person too difficult for one or more reasons. Perhaps the disability causes severe frustration for you, perhaps there is a conflict in personality—whatever the reason, request a change, quietly and confidentially.

The following tips may make the teaching task a bit easier:

- Remember that everyone has a disability of one sort or another—some are just more visible.

- Be positive—attitude is important to the success of the program.

- Be friendly and understanding and explore mutual interests. When students ask questions, answer the questions as directly and completely as you can. If you don't know the answer, say so.

- Be sensitive, but show empathy, not sympathy.

- Relax. If it's difficult to know what to do or say, let the disabled person put you at ease. Discuss the disability in a normal fashion, taking your cue from the individual.

- Learn about participants' needs, abilities, and disabilities. Explore the group's interests.

- Learn about the characteristics of certain conditions and diseases, keeping in mind that they often have no set course or limitation. Be aware of activity guidelines prescribed for the individuals in your class.

- Be considerate. Speak directly to a person with a disability, not through a family member or nondisabled friend or peer. Don't lean on anyone's wheelchair or equipment while talking.

- Allow enough time to finish a task, whether in the locker room or in the swim area. Let the person with the disability set the pace in walking or talking.

- Teach basic movements but adapt them to individual ability. Keep progressions simple.

- Use the three Rs—routine, repetition, and relaxation.

- Speak to each student directly, clearly, and with eye contact. For those who have difficulty speaking, ask questions that require short answers or a shake of the head. For those who have difficulty hearing, speak slowly and distinctly. Use gestures to communicate, and when necessary, write a short note.

- Be firm but patient.

- Be enthusiastic and praise often. Keep classes fun!

- Build success experiences into your lessons, at least one per session.

- Seek out and learn from resource people available to you. This would include health care professionals, people in organizations for special populations, and college and university experts.

- Allow participants to keep prosthetic devices and aids, including wheelchairs and crutches, within reach.

- Ask the individual how best to assist and make it easy and comfortable. When possible, let the student ask for assistance. Respect the person's right to indicate what help is needed. Don't ignore an obvious need, but don't overdo assistance.

- Be aware of unusual situations and obstacles that impede communication and participation, such as poor lighting and acoustics. Think *safety*.

- Maintain strict confidentiality at all times about personal information or medical records that you have access to as you teach.

Teaching Swimming to Special Populations

Although each student must be considered individually, there are common issues related to the specific disabilities of each population. The following sections, covering those with physical disabilities, sensory disabilities, mental disabilities, mental retardation, learning disabilities, and problems due to aging, provide some helpful information on working with these groups. More information on specific disabilities is available in chapter 7.

Working With the Physically Disabled

Some of the most common types of physical disabilities seen in aquatics programs are cerebral palsy, multiple sclerosis, and muscular dystrophy. Accident victims also compose a substantial number of program participants. A physical disability often is secondary to a psychological disability. The ability to live with reduced physical functions is particularly difficult for teenagers and young adults.

Swim skills should be directed toward working with affected muscles and improving muscle tone in the areas adjacent to them. Similar methods may be employed when working with spastic and paralytic participants. The ability of the student to coordinate movements and concentrate on what is expected is critical.

When working with a swimmer weak in an upper extremity or with involvement of one side of the body, teach symmetrical movements and strokes starting from a supine position, such as the back float, and adjust the swimmer's body by depressing the shoulder or placing the arm or leg so that balance is achieved. Students should begin with forward and backward gliding; then try finning, winging, and sculling on the back; and when feasible, add the breast. Asymmetrical strokes such as the crawl are difficult to master and should be taught at a later date. Swimmers with involvement on one side of the body may find a scissors kick easy to learn; arm movements, such as finning, sculling, and winging, can be added.

A student with only one arm or leg may have difficulty balancing in the water. When teaching a float or glide, use a flotation device on the impaired side to compensate for the missing limb. After the student achieves balance, the flotation device may be eliminated. A backcrawl or adaptation of the elementary backstroke also can be taught. When a leg is affected, the student should work from the glide to a sidestroke position. If both legs have been lost, the student should be taught to propel on his or her back. An overarm stroke in the prone position with rotary breathing helps develop a simulated sidestroke.

Physical conditions do not limit a person from adapting many skills successfully, attaining confidence, and enjoying and being safe in the water.

Working With Those With Sensory Disabilities

Sensory disabilities include hearing impairments, deafness, visual impairments, blindness, or a combination of deafness and blindness. Each type requires certain adjustments in instruction.

Few people with impaired hearing are totally deaf; most can hear some sound. The extent of hearing loss will vary from individual to individual. Those who are deaf but who once had hearing are easier to work with than those who have been deaf from birth. Use manual movements rather than sounds in teaching this group. A knowledge of sign language is helpful, and in some cases an interpreter may be required. Some hearing impaired people also have balance and perceptual motor difficulties, and in such cases understanding and patience are necessary to help them adjust to the aquatic environment.

More than half of those people considered blind actually have partial vision, but even those who are totally blind can benefit from water activities. Aquatics helps those with visual disabilities acquire skills that help them integrate into society. Use verbalization and kinesthetic demonstration rather than visual instruction.

Loss of vision in one eye is a disability that presents particular problems. People with this disability may have a loss of both three-dimensional vision and a sense of equilibrium. Through balancing exercises and swimming, they can improve these faculties.

When people with visual impairments are brought to the aquatics area for the first time, orient them to all facilities, such as the locker room, bathrooms, and pool (shallow and deep ends). This orientation should precede any work in the water. They need to know where various objects are, such as the sides of the pool or ropes, and the origin of various sounds. Always announce your identity by speaking first so they feel at ease. Use physical guidance, such as letting them hold your arm while walking or guiding their arms and legs when demonstrating skills, to help them participate and learn.

People who are both deaf and blind often find that aquatic activities aid their emotional and social growth and development, provide interaction with the world, offer opportunities to improve communications skills and learn motor development skills, and assist in their rehabilitation. These people are frequently isolated and may exhibit inappropriate behavior such as fear, withdrawal, hyperexcitability, and emotional stress. To counteract this, physically guide them so they can explore their environment. Trust must be developed before progress can be made. Once water adjustment and security have been established, add swimming aids to provide new opportunities for independence in the water. In teaching swimming, as in teaching other motor development or learning tasks, follow a sequenced pattern of skills. When working with those who are deaf and blind, keep sufficiently close to them to make them aware of your presence.

Working With the Mentally Disabled

While a person with mental disabilities has the same basic needs as anyone else in aquatics, he or she may require special consideration, understanding, and care.

Experiment with visual, verbal, and abstract stimuli in class. Simple explanations and demonstrations, while important to the learning process, may not always be sufficient. Guided movement and the opportunity to feel may be more important. Sensory awareness, hearing, smelling, and touching are necessary for some students; multisensory approach may work.

To physically assist students, use flotation devices to support the trunk of the body as well as the limbs. These devices assist with balance and endurance and allow students to gain confidence in the water more quickly. If possible, the aquatics program should be coordinated with a gym program designed to meet the needs of the participant. Games and music work especially well with those who are mentally disabled. The rhythm of music can be matched easily to the rhythm of a stroke.

Working with the emotionally disturbed person requires patience and understanding. The disturbed person is not unwilling to conform but is simply unable to do so. He or she should be permitted to speak out in anger without being harshly censured. Reacting aggressively to aggressive behavior will not meet the needs of the student; ask those who work with the emotionally disturbed person what the best way is to handle such behavior.

Working With the Mentally Retarded

Physical activity in the water is highly effective for working with the participant who is mentally retarded. Water activity offers habilitation and rehabilitation in many ways.

Success develops individuals' self-respect and ability for self-expression. Many people who are mentally retarded experience their first measure of success in a water program. Achieving even the simplest skill and being reinforced for it can be exciting. To walk alone in the water may be the most important thing in the world for those who have multiple disabilities.

Aquatics can also develop physical abilities and fitness. The person who is physically disabled as well as retarded can learn movements that improve coordination not only in the water, but also on land. For example, walking, hopping, skipping, crawling, and kicking as well as laterality and directionality are stressed in the water. For the able-bodied as well as the disabled, aquatics builds strength and endurance and promotes better health. Specific skills are learned, such as water safety and survival swimming, movement through the water, and coordination of body movements.

In addition, aquatics provides an opportunity for development of rhythm and movement. Movement exploration in the water can be educational as well as fun. Aquatics activities may present opportunities to teach the meaning and pronunciation of new vocabulary. It also may aid in the development of visual perception; the use of shapes and formations can be part of a water program. Even color discrimination, numbers, and other traditional classroom subjects may be taught through aquatics. For instance, students may be asked to relate their experiences to the class or describe their feelings in some other way.

Aquatics can add to the personal skills of those who are mentally retarded. A water program can assist in the development of social awareness. Acceptable behavior in a pool situation is a must. Individuals must become aware of the needs of other class members in order to participate. It provides an opportunity for them to be part of a group in an acceptable manner, which may then carry over to other group settings. Group games also create situations in which appropriate behavior during group activities can be learned.

Personal adjustment is also encouraged by aquatics. Special aquatic events may offer the person who is retarded his or her first chance to be included in fun activities. Aquatics may improve the individual's mental outlook by providing an outside interest. This interest may help the person use leisure time more effectively, as the person who swims can accompany his or her family in swimming or join in school or community swim groups. The utlimate goal always is to integrate the special program into the "normal" program.

It is impossible to separate recreation, education, and rehabilitation when speaking of a program for the mentally retarded. The YMCA provides educational opportunities for the individual through the development of physical activities. Aquatics is no exception; it is a tool or vehicle through which to teach the individual. The end result should be one of habilitation. Almost all mentally retarded children and adults can achieve in the water. Due to lack of opportunity, many of these people have not participated in aquatic activities, and their performance initially is poor. However, when work in the water is coordinated with a gym program that improves movement and coordination, the gap in performance between that of the person who is retarded and the "normal" person is substantially and quickly reduced.

Skills are perfected according to ability. The first goal is learning water safety, the second is perfecting skills. Competition in Special Olympics and other games offers a new challenge in aquatics for the individual who is retarded. Swimming, including water safety, and other areas of aquatics may give new value and meaning to the lives of those who are mentally retarded. The development of social, auditory, visual, speech, and motor skills is all part of "water learning."

Some participants may be mildly disabled. Those labeled as educable mentally retarded, learning disabled, behaviorally disordered, emotionally disturbed, and educationally handicapped may have minor disabilities. Such participants are relatively common in any given population. They may be identified as disabled only during their school years; they usually lead productive lives, marry, support themselves, and blend completely into society. Teaching aquatics skills to these participants is much the same as instructing regular program participants. No special equipment or facilities are needed, but kickboards and flotation devices may be helpful.

Mildly disabled participants probably have experienced failure more frequently than their peers. Failure to learn as others do often causes them to be referred and diagnosed as having special needs. These participants should be guaranteed success in learning any task; success can be assured by starting with skills they already have mastered. From there, they should progress in small, sequential steps toward the same goals as nondisabled participants. Small classes, repetition, drills, and smiles of encouragement help the individual with a minor disability learn to swim.

Equipment can help a mildly disabled child or adult learn more quickly. PFDs can provide extra support for people afraid of the water. Fins can help with kicking and gradually can be phased out as the person develops a stronger kick. Flotation devices can be made from empty plastic gallon bleach or milk jugs that have been rinsed well and sealed, and towels may be used as tow ropes to help students learn to glide. Plastic jugs filled with sand may be used as weights to be recovered from the pool bottom; they can be wrapped in aluminum foil for added visibility. Ping-Pong balls blown across the pool can be used for teaching breathing techniques.

Working With the Learning Disabled

Learning disabilities are perceptual, conceptual, or subtle coordinative disorders that interfere with learning. The causes of learning disabilities are unknown. Most experts believe they are caused by illness or injury during pregnancy or during or just after birth. Some may be hereditary. Learning disabilities are often hidden, and individuals may not be aware of such problems or be understanding about them. Many people with learning disabilities, however, have succeeded in sports, business, government, and community affairs.

People with learning disabilities have difficulty understanding or processing oral or visual information. This may cause social problems as well as learning problems, as they may not observe what is going on around them and thus may not get along well with others. The way that information is presented to people with learning disabilities is very important. They may not always remember what they have heard, but they do seem to be able to retain what they have experienced. This concept must be extended into the learning disabled person's total life if that person is to avoid becoming so frustrated with others that he or she develops emotional, social, and family problems.

For some people who are learning disabled, swimming may provide a challenging way to develop gross motor strength. New experiences can be frightening to those with learning disabilities, but most of them have found water activities to be enjoyable. In the water there is an opportunity for individually initiated activities and movement. With practice such students are able to achieve the required skills. However, they need patient, thoughtful, and understanding instruction. Always ask such students to repeat instructions given, as they may not have heard what has been said. They may also need additional supervision if they are distractible or hyperactive. If so, develop ways in which to maintain continual contact with them.

Working With the Elderly

As the general population continues to age, more and more adults are participating in physical fitness programs, including aquatics. Chronological age can be misleading; functional age is more important to health and well-being. While certain characteristics and changes are an inevitable part of the aging process, many people may be physically and mentally fit and active well into their eighth or ninth decade of life. However, others may be quite frail beginning at midlife. Nutrition, fitness, and life-style play important roles in the aging process. Some illnesses of aging, such as osteoporosis, may be preventable through proper exercise and calcium-rich diets.

Older adults who are fit usually prefer to participate in regular YMCA aquatics programs. The frail elderly may wish to enroll in aquatics programs that are less strenuous and specifically designed for them.

Aquatics may benefit both the active and the frail older adult. Physical benefits of aquatics can include improved flexibility, muscle strength, endurance, cardiovascular endurance, balance, coordination, and ability. Psychological benefits can include increased self-confidence, self-esteem, stability, sense of achievement, acceptance by others, expression of feelings, and recognition of creative abilities, as well as decreased depression.

Just as important as physical and psychological benefits are social benefits, which may be the primary reason for an older adult to join a program. Social benefits can include increased contact with others; a chance to form new friendships; decreased isolation, loneliness, and boredom; and increased sharing, emotional support, tactile contact, cooperation, and fun.

When working with the frail elderly some precautions should be taken. Fragile bones and delicate skin should be protected, which may mean particular care in getting into and out of the pool as well as in the pool, shower, and dressing area. Those with Alzheimer's disease or senile dementia should be carefully attended, as they may be unable to follow directions and may try to leave the pool area during class.

Communication with older people with sensory disabilities is the same as communication with younger people who are visually or hearing impaired. Hearing aids are taken off before entering the pool, so older people who hear well with aids may have some difficulty in the pool area. Some older people may be reluctant to admit to a hearing problem; speak clearly and maintain direct contact with them. The visually handicapped initially may need to work with a "buddy." They should be familiarized thoroughly with the building and aquatics area. The environment should be completely hazard free; sound or sight "landmarks" should be placed in strategic locations.

Older people attending aquatics classes as part of a rehabilitation regimen after a heart attack or stroke should strictly adhere to their physician's recommendations. If they feel they can undertake more strenuous exercise, they must obtain their physician's permission to do so.

Many YMCAs already have programs for older adults, but even without one community outreach will increase program participation in aquatics. Community members, nursing home residents, church members, and other program participants may wish to join YMCA aquatics individually or with their group. Instructors in Y programs working with older adults should be well trained and enjoy working with older people. Many older participants choose the YMCA as the site for their aquatics and fitness programs because they are treated as individuals and shown genuine care and concern.

Games for Children
With Disabilities

Teaching with a playful attitude is effective and fun. There are several types of games that have their place in children's programs—permissive games and fantasy games; music and rhythm; stunts; relays; tag games; games involving win/lose competition; and the nobody wins, nobody loses new games. Equipment such as flotation devices and kickboards can be helpful and add to a student's pleasure and independent accomplishment. When choosing games, remember the following basic safety skills:

- Front float and recovery
- Back float and recovery
- Blowing and breath control
- Turning over
- Changing direction

Following are some lists of informal games that should spark spontaneity and imagination, designed as a take-off point for working with disabled preschoolers and young students. A game may be played on many different levels but listed only once. For example, under "General Body Movement," a train game is listed; it can progress to hand-over-hand movement then to swimming a beginning stroke along the "track." Remember to choose games appropriate to the children's age.

Water Adjustment

- Washing your face: with two hands, gently splashing face
- Taking a bath: washing face, neck, arms, legs, and body
- Playing catch with a ball: instructor in water, child sitting on edge of pool
- Taxi ride: instructor giving child a piggyback ride; child holding onto neck, feet around waist
- Pass the kickboard: standing in group circle, passing kickboard around, start and finish with instructor
- Washing machine: putting hands on hips, swishing through water with torso twist

Bubbles

- Birthday candles: blowing out pretend candles, blowing bubbles in water
- Pretend bubble pipe: blowing bubbles as if with a bubble pipe
- Straw: using real soda straw or pretend one to blow bubbles
- Blowing a hole in the water: by blowing just above water level, displacing water in shape of a hole
- Blowing a Ping-Pong ball: along gutter or across pool, competition or individual skill
- Blowing off steam: while pretending to be a train, placing hands on pool gutter or edge, stretching out arms and legs, blowing bubbles in water

- Talking to Mr. Fish: blowing bubbles to talk, placing ear in water to listen
- Peek-a-boo: putting head in water on call of "peek" pulling head out of water on call of "boo"
- Pretending to blow up balloons: blowing as if into a balloon
- Blowing a whistle: pretending to have a whistle, blowing bubbles atop water as if blowing a whistle
- Big Bad Wolf: puffing out checks and saying, "He blew and he blew and he blew the house down"
- Frog Face: puffing out cheeks, blowing bubbles, and saying "ribet"

Whole Self Wet

- While asking who can get their chins wet, dipping chin in water—same with cheek
- Number games: counting aloud while students' faces are submerged
- *Hokey Pokey*: playing the singing game *Hokey Pokey* in a circle:

  > *You put your right hand in,*
  > *You put your right hand out,*
  > *You put your right hand in,*
  > *And you shake it all about.*
  > *You do the hokey pokey*
  > *And you turn yourself around.*
  > *And that's what it's all about.*

  (Sing verses in sequence: left hand, right foot, left foot, head, whole self.)

- *Ring Around the Rosie*: playing the singing game *Ring Around the Rosie* in a circle:

  > *Ring around the rosie,*
  > *Pocket full of posie,*
  > *Ashes, ashes,*
  > *We all fall down (or up).*

  (Students hold hands and sing as song is acted out.)

- *Ten Little Indians*: playing the singing game *Ten Little Indians* in a row:

    > *One little, two little, three little Indians,*
    > *Four little, five little, six little Indians,*
    > *Seven little, eight little, nine little Indians,*
    > *Ten little Indian boys (or girls).*

    (Students bob under or jump off wall as instructor counts.)

- *London Bridge*: playing the singing game *London Bridge* in a row:

    > *London Bridge is falling down,*
    > *Falling down, falling down.*
    > *London Bridge is falling down,*
    > *My fair lady (or gentleman).*

    The instructor and a partner are facing each other, holding hands to form a bridge under which students pass. At the end of the song, the bridge is lowered to catch the student underneath.

- *Follow the Leader*: students in circle or line; instructor is leader first in performing a trick or skill, everyone following and imitating leader; another becomes leader and so on.

- *Through the Hoop*: holding a hula hoop on the surface for students to swim through, lowering the hoop gradually so students swim deeper

General Body Movement

- Gas station: students pretending to be boats or cars that need gas follow leader to various points around pool (such as along wall) that are "gas stations"; a kickboard on the edge of a gutter may be the gas pump, a bubble strap may be a hose
- Train: making choo-choo sounds while moving around the pool gutter, holding on with two hands; making chug-chug sounds, first adding a kick, then one hand doing the dog paddle motion as a wheel; then blowing off steam, holding the gutter with two hands and blowing bubbles

- Slalom: swimming around objects or persons
- Obstacle course: swimming around or through objects such as hula hoops during a distance swim
- Red Light, Green Light: swimming until leader says "red light," stopping, then starting on green light announcement

Kicking

- Motor boat: acting as a boat, kicking feet, which are the motor, up and down to splash; swimming by pulling kickboard or floating on own
- Rev engines: kicking faster
- Herman Munster running: running across pool like Herman Munster, not bending the knees; then kicking on front with Herman Munster straight legs
- Losing knees: while learning to flutter kick on back, hiding the knees by keeping them straight and under water
- Getting the people watching wet: kicking forcefully while holding onto the side of the pool
- Making a peanut butter sandwich: doing the backfloat, using the kickboard as bread held flat against the stomach, which is peanut butter; splashing feet as in flutter kick
- Making a fountain: in backfloat position, doing a splashing flutter kick
- Bouncing a pretend ball on toes: in backfloat position doing a splashing flutter kick

Backfloat

- Airplane: lying on back, spreading arms out as the wings of a plane
- Letter "T": lying on back, arms outspread, feet together, in the shape of a "T"
- Nap on a mattress: floating on top of instructor doing backfloat

Finning

- Big Bird: flapping small finning-size wings under water as Big Bird

- Rowboat: making small finning motions to propel self while pretending to be a boat (may sing the song "Row, Row, Row Your Boat" as well)
- Five Little Chickadees: finning away from the edge of the pool one by one as instructor repeats "Five little chickadees hanging on the wall, one flew (jumped) off and then there were four" (numbers drop by one with each repetition)

Dogpaddle Arms

- Sand scooping: pulling hand through water as if scooping up sand
- Digging for a bone: pulling hands alternately through water like a dog digging for a bone
- Water whoosh: feeling the "whoosh" of water pass as hand moves through water
- Climbing ladder: moving hands alternately as if going up a ladder, hands remaining under water
- Feeling Jell-O move: pretending hand is a spoon moving through a big bowl of Jell-O (the water), pulling hard because the Jell-O goes back together

Diving

- Humpty Dumpty: sitting on the side of the pool, everyone repeats "Humpty Dumpty"; as "fall" is said, the instructor guides one student at a time into a beginning sitting dive
- Diving for treasure: sitting on the side of the pool, students are guided one at a time into a beginning sitting dive to look for pretend buried treasure at the pool bottom
- Bunny ears: sitting on the edge of the pool with feet held against the side of the pool, knees spread, arms up around ears, and hands above head; students are each guided into headfirst water entry
- Teapot: assuming the position described for Bunny ears, pretending to be a teapot pouring tea into a cup between the knees at water level (achieves body rotation and headfirst entry)

Jumping

- Milk shake: sitting on the edge of the pool, children are asked what kind of milk shake each wants to be; they then jump in one at a time and spin around to mix the milk shake.
- Burger: sitting on the edge of the pool, children listen as the instructor explains that they are hamburgers, that hamburgers cook in a skillet, and that the water beneath them is that skillet. They then jump in one at a time, choosing to cook on the front or back first, then turning on the other side to cook. The instructor applies pretend catsup and students gobble each other up.

Front Survival Float

- Toe touching: hanging in the water, holding the breath, trying to touch toes under water
- Rag doll: hanging in the water, pretending to be Raggedy Ann or Raggedy Andy
- Marionette: floating while instructor holds pretend strings in middle of students' backs
- Dishrag: pretending to be an old, wet, floppy dishrag, hanging in the water as for toe touching

Bobbing

- Jack-in-the-box: Pretending to be jack-in-the-boxes, blowing bubbles in the pool when inside the box, then popping up to get a breath
- Elevator: Pretending to ride an elevator while holding pool edge, riding up to the third floor then down under water to the basement (while under water, blowing bubbles)
- Pop Goes the Weasel: singing the song and going under to blow at "Pop Goes the Weasel."
- Pop-up toaster: pretending to be toast, blowing bubbles when down, popping up for a new breath
- Hiccups: pretending to have hiccups, blowing out when under water, coming up for a new breath when hiccuping

Rotary Breathing

- Old man snoring: pretending to snore, taking a breath in with head to side, snoring and blowing bubbles out with head in water
- Talking to Mr. Fish: talking to Mr. Fish, who lives under water, by blowing out; listening to him with the ear that always stays in the water while taking a new breath
- Hi, Tinkie: with a waterproof happy face bandage on the upper arm of each student on the breathing side (or waterproof drawing of a happy face), saying "Hi, Tinkie" every time the face is seen (head turned for new breath)

Lifesaving Skill

- Man overboard: pretending someone fell out of a boat, throwing a kickboard to help him
- Catch the ball: throwing a ball to a student, who uses it to float

Backcrawl Arms

- Helicopter: pretending arms are the rotors turning to help swim
- Row, Row, Row Your Boat: singing while doing backcrawl armstroke
- Hiding elbows: keeping elbows straight while doing armstroke

Front Float Glide

- Nap on tummy: lying on front and relaxing, face in
- Torpedo/zoom: pushing off from side of pool, face in, or being pushed off by instructor
- Glass bottom boat: pretending to be a glass bottom boat, seeing pretty fish under water

Total Lesson

Imaginatively plan a total 30-minute lesson on one of the following themes, moving around the pool and pacing students in an effective learning situation. For example, an activity can include swimming down the lane to visit "Grandma's apartment" using a car or other transportation; arriving there and using an elevator; getting a grocery list and traveling back to the other end of the pool to a pretend grocery store where groceries are selected; placing the pretend items on kickboards and traversing the pool again; and finally delivering the groceries.

- Birthday party
- Treasure hunt
- Taking a trip
- Going to store for Grandma
- Big Bad Wolf (use story)
- Bus ride to go Christmas shopping
- Bear Hunt (use story)
- Beauty shop
- Playground
- Picnic or campout
- Parade (being motorcycles, trucks, fire trucks, etc.)

Marching in a Circle

The following songs are suitable for older students and may be found in old-fashioned folksong books.

- Glory, Glory Hallelujah
- When the Saints Go Marching In
- Goodnight Irene
- You Are My Sunshine
- I've Been Working on the Railroad
- Bicycle Built for Two

Singing Group Games

The following songs are found in children's songbooks.

- Bingo
- Farmer in the Dell
- Hokey Pokey
- Here We Go Round the Mulberry Bush
- Looby Loo

- Motor Boat
- People on the Bus
- Pop Goes the Weasel
- Rig a Jig Jig
- Ring Around the Rosie
- Row, Row, Row Your Boat
- Sandyland

Recognition and Awards

Recognition may well be the keystone to participant success and pleasure. It is also vitally important for volunteers, instructors, and cooperating agencies. Families who help by offering time and assistance and those who simply go to the YMCA for special events often enjoy recognition as well.

Participant recognition can be in the form of ribbons, pins, patches, and skill sheets marked with accomplishments. (Recognition forms are available for YMCAs through the Program Store.) Students enjoy receiving something tangible to mark progress and accomplishments. When possible, give recognition and rewards at the moment of success. Recognize and reward the daily successes—perhaps with an inexpensive toy, a treat, a warm smile, or words of praise—as well as the long-term successes.

Goals for Instructors

A central goal of programming for special populations is creating attitudes and feelings of acceptance. The modification of both instructors' and students' attitudes and feelings is one of the most difficult tasks in education. Both positive and negative attitudes are learned by imitation, often during the early years of life. However, even negative attitudes can be changed through sensitization. Sensitivities are learned through living, and each of us must do our own examining and changing.

Class periods can become a "living laboratory experience" in which each student has an opportunity to be happily and deeply himself or herself. Students may have negative and fearful feelings as well as positive and social feelings. Instructors should accept all these feelings and show warmth and caring to each student. Teachers should also be dependable and mean what they say. They should create a safe climate of unconditional positive feelings for each student. When the feelings are genuine and instructors are positive and empathetic, students sense this and may be able to

- see themselves in a different, more positive way;
- accept themselves and their feelings more fully;
- become more self-confident and self-directing;
- become more flexible and less rigid;
- adopt more realistic goals;
- behave more maturely;
- change maladjusted behavior;
- accept others;
- become open to what is going on outside as well as inside themselves; and
- change basic personality characteristics in constructive ways.

The aquatics instructor of students with special needs is in an excellent position to nurture students' creativity, independence, and self-confidence. Instructors can create an atmosphere in which attitudes and feelings may improve.

Health and Safety 4

Health and safety factors are always important in aquatics programs, but many additional safeguards are necessary when working with special populations. Care must be taken to ensure safety when disabled students are in the locker room or entering or leaving the pool, especially when they are trying to move from one area to another. Extra safety and health precautions are also needed that take students' disabilities into consideration.

Moving in the Locker Room and Pool Area Safely

Many students with restricted mobility will need assistance in moving from place to place in the locker room and from the locker room to the pool.

Moving Student From Wheelchair to Toilet or Chair

When moving a hemiplegic student, place the wheelchair in front of and facing the toilet and leave sufficient space for turning. When necessary, help the student push to a standing position where he or she can reach for the toilet seat with the functional hand, pivot, and sit. When the student needs to return to the wheelchair, the procedure should be reversed. The student's weak leg should be between the helper's legs, with the inside of the helper's leg positioned to lock the student's knee into extension with the helper's knee when the student stands.

When moving a paraplegic student, place the wheelchair alongside the toilet (or commode chair with removable armrest) or at a 45-degree angle to the toilet. Remove the wheelchair armrests and swing the footrests out of the way. The student can transfer by pushing up with one hand on the toilet seat and the other on the wheelchair. Clothing should be adjusted before the transfer from the wheelchair and after returning to the wheelchair. Because of balance problems, an assisted transfer may be necessary, which requires one person to lift and place the student's legs and another behind the wheelchair to lift and place the trunk. The helper should place his or her arms beneath the student's armpits, grasping the forearms, folding them across the student's chest, and hugging them to the chest. The two-person team should carefully coordinate efforts, minimizing jarring movements.

A quadriplegic student often needs a commode chair with swing-away or removable armrests. Transfer can be done in the same way as for the paraplegic student.

Moving From Wheelchair to Shower

Amputees and hemiplegic students usually can be assisted in much the same ways. Often the student will need a seat; those with balance problems should have a backrest. A shower railing or safety handle may be the only accommodation necessary.

Paraplegic students may find showering easier if the shower is equipped with a shower chair with removable armrests. Quadriplegic students can use a commode chair with removable armrests. The ledge in many stall showers may be an obstacle, and accommodations must be made.

Moving From Wheelchair to Deck

Amputees and hemiplegic students may need no assistance at all, but if they do, the following procedure can be used: From a standing position, the student's hips and knees are bent so that the center of gravity is as close to the deck as possible. The student reaches for the deck with the unaffected hand and side, sitting toward the uninvolved side and taking care not to fall toward the spastic or affected side.

Paraplegic students can be assisted in the following ways: For one procedure a series of graduated stools is placed in front of the wheelchair, and the helper puts the student's legs on the stools. The student does sitting push-ups, lowering himself or herself down the stools one at a time. In another procedure, a wooden chair is placed beside the wheelchair. The wheelchair armrests are removed, and the student does a sitting push-up with one hand on the wooden chair and one on the wheelchair, lowering himself or herself to the deck. One other method for students with good balance and body control is bending over, keeping one hand on the deck and the other on the wheelchair seat, and doing a sitting push-up to the deck.

Entering and Exiting the Pool Safely

A major problem in aquatics programs is access to the pool. To help an individual get into a pool of any type, first get his or her suggestions. People with disabilities deal with many types of barriers every day and may well have some innovative approaches for their specific needs. The following are some examples:

- Bring the participant into the pool on a litter and let the person float off, giving only the assistance necessary.
- Use a wide board on which the participant can slide into or gradually enter the pool backward or forward as independently as possible.
- Have the participant scoot into the pool from wide steps.
- Take a waterproof wheelchair, shower chair, or toilet chair directly down a ramp or wide steps into the pool, then let the participant move or be helped from the chair into the water.
- Carry a small child piggyback into the pool.
- Adapt one-, two-, three-, and four-person first aid carries to physically lift and carry participants into and out of the pool.
- Roll the participant from the top of the ledge into the water.

- Use poly-gym mats or foam mats to expedite participants' entry and exit.
- Purchase a portable ramp to meet specific needs or for specific pools.
- Build a platform near the side or wall of the pool so the participant can bring a wheelchair to it, move from the chair to the platform, and get into the water.
- Build a ramp on one side of an outdoor pool so the seat of the wheelchair at the ramp end is even with the pool side for easy transfer.

The following are specific ways in which pools have been made more accessible:

- A pool has been built that is 6 feet deep, 2 feet above and 4 feet below the ground, for a polio quadriplegic. The pool bottom gradually slopes up to 2 feet at the center so that when swimmers want to exit, they simply go to the shallowest part, sit on the edge of the pool, and have someone turn their legs around and transfer them back to their wheelchair.
- A 25-by-40-foot pool used by a Florida hospital has a ramp 4 feet wide and 21 feet long, sloping down at the shallow end. Handrails flank both sides of the ramp, and a winch is mounted on a wall opposite the ramp that can be hooked to a wheelchair, permitting someone to lower or pull out a person unable to walk.
- A monorail system in conjunction with a truck hoist and special chair is used by a YMCA in Longview, Washington, because the pool decks are too narrow to permit passage of a wheelchair along the edge of the pool from the dressing rooms to the desired point of entry into the water. The swimmer is placed in the special chair at the dressing room door, secured with a safety belt, lifted approximately 2 inches above the floor by the hoist, and pushed horizontally along the pool edge. A pool attendant manipulates the ropes or chains on the hoist and lowers the swimmer until the chair rests on the bottom of the pool. The safety belt is unfastened and the swimmer is assisted from the chair. The sequence is reversed when the swimmer leaves the pool.

General Safety Precautions

In any aquatics program, safety procedures should be taught to staff and participants at the beginning of each session and reinforced daily. They should include the following:

- Teach all students how to get in and out of the pool in an emergency; staff assistance may be needed. For example, three short whistles can mean "clear the pool." Practice and use emergency procedures with discretion.
- Prepare and file incident reports carefully.
- Make certain a trained lifeguard is on deck, regardless of the student-teacher ratio. Program safety and students' abilities determine the ratio. Guards should be experienced at getting disabled people in and out of the water; they should know which participants are most likely to need assistance and watch them carefully.
- Train staff and lifeguards in CPR, first aid, and procedures for aiding participants having seizures.
- Prepare warmer water for beginning swimmers and for most people who have disabilities. Water temperatures of 83 degrees and above are recommended for people with special needs.

The following are some general safety precautions that should always be taken:

- Make certain the student always knows what you are trying to do. Stabilize or lock all equipment, furniture, wheelchairs, and devices to prevent tipping, slipping, or moving. Safety belts or their equivalent facilitate handling students while ensuring safety in the performance of the task.
- Be prepared to prevent falls. Make certain no sharp obstacles are in the vicinity, and learn the proper procedures for reporting accidents.
- Take care not to bump the limbs or feet of paralyzed people. Their skin can break down easily and decubitus sores can form. These students may need to wear socks for protection, and caution should be taken during entry into and exit from the pool as well as during pool activities.
- Take care not to cause bone injuries. A characteristic of certain disabilities is fragile, easily broken or fractured bones.

Because of osteoporosis, the frail elderly may be vulnerable to breaks and fractures.

- Know how to transfer students of any type and size. For protection, always keep fundamental body mechanics in mind when lifting or transferring someone. Stay close to the center of gravity of the part or person being moved. Maintain a straight spine and bent knees and use your legs rather than your back to lift, move, or hold a load. For safety, instruct another person in how best to help in transferring participants.

Health Considerations

To ensure that participants are comfortable and safe during classes, the following points should be considered.

Pool.   Often water temperature in classes for people with special needs is 83 degrees or higher. Warm temperatures increase the opportunity for bacterial growth, so water should be chlorinated, filtered, and checked often to ensure proper chemistry. An adequate turnover of water, depending on the bather load, is essential. The pool should have a good filter-purification system and, when possible, a heating system capable of raising water temperatures quickly. In a multipurpose pool, consider using some method of bulkheading, placing dividing walls within the pool to efficiently raise pool temperature in the instructional or therapeutic areas. Every region of the country has its own health regulations; ask the health department pertinent questions.

Whirlpools and hot tubs.   While whirlpools and hot tubs are wonderful relaxation aids, bacteria grow rapidly because of the heat and movement of the water. These facilities must be monitored carefully and checked frequently. They should only be used with a physician's consent and generally are counterindicated for people with heart conditions, young children, pregnant women, and people with multiple sclerosis, for whom heat may be debilitating.

Air temperature.   Ideally, air temperature and flow should be controlled to prevent evaporation chilling when a student leaves the water. A place for hanging towels and robes should be provided in the pool area so students are dry and warm when on deck. Radiant heat has been installed in some pool ceilings; a good location is above the waiting area, where towels and robes also can be left.

Incontinence. Some students may be incontinent, and precautions should be taken to prevent urine or fecal matter from entering the pool. Swimmers may use special rubber pants with tight-fitting leg bands; many are very careful about preventing potentially embarrassing situations. Catheters and colostomy bags should be clamped off during pool time. Appropriate containers should be available in the dressing and bathroom areas for diapers, colostomy bags, and other such items.

Emergency plans. All aquatics facilities should have an emergency pool evacuation plan. Practice emergency procedures regularly and post emergency numbers clearly. Swimmers who cannot hear whistles or see warning signs should have a buddy or volunteer who lets them know when they must leave the pool, get to safety, or take whatever action is necessary.

Medical treatment. Some swimmers may be using various drugs and medications; others may have disabilities with such symptoms as seizures or loss of consciousness. Review participants' health records regularly to be aware of new drugs, prescribed drug side effects, new symptoms, or any physical changes. Speak to physicians, families, professional personnel at institutions, school officials, and participants as frequently as necessary to protect student safety. Staff members oriented to safety and health considerations who have recently completed CPR and first aid updates and understand the possible effects of medication and treatment of seizures, asthma attacks, dizziness, and other conditions should successfully cope with any special situation. Only qualified people should be assigned to dispense medication to individuals; medication should be secured in a place handy to the pool.

The disabilities considered in this book are not contagious. People with infections, illnesses, or open sores, or who might otherwise endanger others, should not participate in aquatics activities.

Leadership 5

A successful aquatics program for those with physical, sensory, or mental disabilities requires the smoothly coordinated efforts of many people. To begin, the person transporting participants to and from the facility must be well trained and the vehicle used for transportation must be insured and safe. The vehicle should be able to accommodate comfortably such equipment as crutches and wheelchairs. The driver must be licensed to handle the vehicle and must know how to assist the participants in entering and exiting it in the safest and most comfortable manner.

Parking at the facility should be clearly marked and easily accessible to the building and pool. Assistance must be available to help participants from vehicle to facility site and may be needed at the aquatics site to help participants dress, undress, and shower. Support staff should know the nature of a participant's disability so that clothing can be changed safely, comfortably, and with dignity.

In the pool, the swimmer is supervised by a program director. If several swimmers are involved at the same time, support staff, including volunteers, should be on hand.

Certain skills, knowledge, and competencies are necessary for a program supervisor to be successful in working with the disabled. These include the following:

- Experience in programs at a pool, camp, beach, agency, or school as an aide, instructor, or supervisor.

- A thorough knowledge of skills and progressions and the ability to break down skills to small steps. Skills should be evaluated on a regular basis.
- An understanding of each participant's specific problems and how the person has adjusted to various disabilities. This helps establish rapport and facilitates individual program planning.
- Ability to communicate with participants—verbally and nonverbally—and to establish rapport.
- Ability to communicate with other support team members including medical and allied medical professionals, school personnel, social workers, parents and families, and other agency personnel. Communication is an ongoing process, and confidentiality is a must.
- Ability to assess and understand specific disabilities and to explain to staff necessary modifications in teaching sequences or methods.
- Training in CPR, first aid, and handling of seizures.
- An understanding of the necessity for continuing pre-service and in-service training.
- Practical experience in using communication aids—hearing aids, sign language—as well as wheelchairs, prosthetic devices, lifts, and transfers.
- Imagination, originality, creativity, and empathy.

Support staff should be selected on the basis of desire to contribute to a successful program and on ability to work well with people who have disabilities. The support staff must perform under the strict instructions of the supervisor. Since detailed records of participants' attitudes, reactions, and progress should be kept and regularly maintained, a single staff member should be responsible for them. A computer can help. The records are particularly valuable in updating individual programs developed for participants as required by Public Law 94-142 (discussed in the next section).

The staff should be in sincere accord with the objectives of the program, the improvement of the physical skills and mental outlook of people with special needs by means of individual and group-tailored experiences in water, either through integrated or segregated programs. Staff members should have the knowledge and expertise to deal effectively with various situations that can arise in an aquatic environment, and safety and emergency procedures must be understood by everyone concerned with the program. Provisions should be made for continued preservice and in-service training for all staff. In addition, all aquatics personnel involved with participants or recordkeeping should be aware of the provisions of Public Law 94-142, a law regarding the education of handicapped children, and how those provisions affect aquatics programs.

Public Law 94-142

The Education for All Handicapped Children Act (PL 94-142), passed in 1975, guarantees six procedural safeguards to protect the rights of children with disabilities and their parents. The safeguards are these:

- Free, appropriate public education must be provided for every child with disabilities between the ages of 3 and 21.
- Due process procedures are guaranteed. These consist of a series of steps to assure the rights of children with disabilities and their parents. Parents must be fully informed and included in any decision regarding the education of their children.
- Nondiscriminatory testing must be given to children to ensure that placement in any special education program is not based solely on any one criterion. Tests and evaluation material must be administered in a way that is neither racially nor culturally discriminatory and must be presented in the native language of the child.
- A "least restrictive environment" must be provided for the individual student. This means that children with disabilities will be educated with nondisabled children to the maximum extent possible. Children with disabilities should be placed in separate or special classes only when the nature or severity of the disability precludes satisfactory education in regular classes.
- Confidentiality of school records is strictly enforced. Any personally identifiable information will be released only with parental permission.
- Appropriate education is ensured by an individualized education program (IEP), a written statement developed for each disabled child by school officials, teachers, parents or guardians, and sometimes the child.

Children who participate in special aquatics programs as a result of special education placement should have an IEP created for them by a support team. This team might include any of the following: special education teachers, regular classroom teachers, resource specialists, principals, physicians, allied medical personnel, therapists, counselors or social workers, program supervisors, water instructors, lifeguards, parents or guardians, physical education instructors, and participants themselves. Special education students should progress from these programs into general programs as soon as possible. This will help them participate in society to the fullest extent possible, as swimming is a recreation skill that helps with socialization as well.

The IEP is a statement or plan for a child with one or more disabilities. By law, it must include the following:

- A description of the child's present performance level— what skills the student already has mastered and what should be mastered.
- Annual goals and expectations based on performance level, which are prioritized on the basis of needs uncovered through assessment and testing.
- Short-term objectives, measurable accomplishments created by dividing the annual goals into small, sequential steps that describe each task the student will complete, how well the task will be completed, and a target date for completion.
- Specific educational services relating to achieving annual goals and meeting individual needs, including transportation, speech therapy, psychological services, medical services, and recreation or any other developmental, supportive, or corrective service necessary. Projected dates of supportive or corrective service necessary. Projected dates of initiation of services and duration of use are required.
- The amount of time the child will participate in the regular classroom and for which activities.
- Objective criteria for each instructional goal. Evaluations are based on whether these goals are reached.
- Person(s) responsible for implementing goals and objectives.

IEPs are developed at a placement advisory committee meeting that includes the people who will implement the plan or be responsible for instruction. Each disabled child is thus assured the best possible individual program. A YMCA that designs and implements aquatics programs for youth with disabilities as part of their "free, appropriate public school education" may be asked to send a representative to help develop the plan. An appropriately trained public schoolteacher or other individual may represent the agency. The IEP is a road map for instruction in all areas for the year and must be reviewed at least annually. The placement advisory committee may be reconvened at the request of any concerned individual (teacher, parent, agency representative, etc.) in contact with the youth. A sample IEP is shown in Figure 1.

In addition to IEPs, some regulatory or certifying bodies may require Individualized Program Plans (IPPs), which include short- and long-term goals, timetables, evaluations, individual accomplishments, and overall program objectives. These program plans are important for such agencies as the YMCA that are seeking funding for aquatics and other activities to serve those with disabilities.

Personnel Requirements

To achieve excellence in programming, aquatics supervisors should consider excellence in the recruitment, selection, and training of personnel. Program planners and supervisors should "think big" from the beginning, building on, complementing, and supplementing existing programs in the wider community, regional, and national areas. Supervisors also should tap into ongoing leadership recruitment, selection, and training. Total program exposure helps in formulating aquatics programs for special populations. Leaders should believe in the YMCA's mission and emphasis on the quality of every life. They should obtain certification in the Basic Aquatic Leadership Course as well as fulfill the requirements of a swim instructor/leader. They also should have individual opportunities to grow, stretch, and further develop marketable skills. Supervising instructors, assistant instructors, and leaders should consider additional certification as instructors/leaders for special populations. Program coordinators should be certified as aquatics instructors or directors.

Lifeguards for pool or waterfront activities need a "third eye." Extra awareness and a thorough knowledge of health concerns

Figure 1. Individualized Education Program: Implementation/Instructional Plan.

Name of
Student _____ Date of Birth _____ Age _____ Grade _____ School _____

Local Education Agency
Name and Phone _____ Date of Entry Into Program _____ Projected Ending Date _____

Signature of Implementor Completing This Form _____

Program Goals	Implementation/Instructional Objectives	Strategies and/or Techniques	Materials and/or Resources	Date Started	Date Ended	Criteria for Mastery of Each Objective
Participation in 4th-grade swimming	Student will enter water un-assisted 100% of the time by November 1, 1986. Teacher will say, "John, come here" once.	1:1 instruction fading out the use of life jacket to enter shallow water on teacher's command.	Life jacket	10/1	11/1	100%
	Student will swim 2 pool lengths (50 yards) without assistance and without touching sides of pool other than to turn.	Individual instruction using physical prompts and lavish praise for skill demonstration; fade out gradually.	Pool grab bar Flotation devices Kickboards	10/1	1/15	2 lengths without assistance 2 consecutive trials
	Student will follow pool rules 95% of the time.	All rules are posted. Every swim day 4th-grade teacher will praise student for all rules followed. Alternative—Student earns 1 point for each swim class where all rules are followed. 20 points earns an extra swim period.	Rules list posted in pool: 1. Walk. 2. Don't bother others. 3. Always swim with a buddy.	10/1		Follows all pool rules for 4 sessions.

and special equipment are essential. In addition to advanced lifesaving and national lifeguard certification, the lifeguard should have taken a course in standard or multimedia first aid and cardiopulmonary resuscitation and the Basic Aquatic Leadership Course, and attended at least one conference, workshop, or extended training on special populations. The lifeguard should know what to expect, be able to assess class participants, and be trained to cope with such concerns as pool accessibility, seizures, cardiac problems, and behavior problems. Guards should be selected for their ability to work under stress. Program coordinators should conduct orientations for lifeguards, and supervising instructors should be responsible for updating guards on special problems.

Supervising Instructor

Supervising instructors should hold a variety of certifications—all those described—the Basic Aquatic Leadership Course, swimming instructor certification, and certification as a specialist instructor for special populations. Supervisors may also hold aquatics instructor or aquatics director ratings. Certification in teaching aquatics for children 5 and under and training in first aid and CPR are recommended, as well as teaching experience in the 5 and under and progressive swimming programs and 100 hours or more experience in aquatics for special populations. Instructors should have maturity and good judgment, plus a sense of humor, enthusiasm, patience, the ability to get along with people of all ages and abilities, talent in keeping records, skill at setting and implementing goals, and ability to constructively critique programs and people. Also important is the ability to reward and recognize teachers, aides, students, and volunteers for attaining goals.

Master Teacher

People who may fall into the category of master teacher are those who have worked continually in aquatics for special populations for a number of years and who have proven their leadership capabilities in teaching, program development, and program implementation. These individuals may be recognized locally or nationally and often become excellent resource people. This is not a certification area but an area of demonstrated ability and knowledge.

Lifeguard

Effective lifeguarding essentially means accident prevention. This includes the following points for all personnel:

- Know the participants. Use current information forms and keep them readily available. All records—attendance, medical information, incident and accident reports, progress reports, records of recognition and awards, and other forms applicable to a program—should be completely updated and easily located for every student.
- Recognize common disabilities. Know their characteristics and what to look for. Students may have obvious problems or may wear medic alert tags. If a disability is difficult to pinpoint, ask the swimmer or attendant about the nature of the disability.
- Know all personnel. Administrators should hire mature, well-informed supervisors and assistant instructors, both paid and volunteer, who know the program and progressions. Clear accountability and communication should be maintained between the program staff and the personnel from institutions and groups involved with the aquatics program.
- Know the facility. Maintain accessibility and know when and where to accommodate and adapt.
- Know safety procedures. Practice them regularly and adapt them when necessary.
- Involve people with special needs in planning and decision making.
- Mainstream whenever possible.
- Promote independence.

People in charge of an aquatics environment must be alert for signs of stress. Reaching safety may be particularly difficult for students with problems such as cramping, spasms, uncontrolled movements in extremities, chills, inability to get rid of water splashed into mouth, and inability to recover from a position in the water. Stress may include chest pain, pain radiating to other extremities, unease and restlessness, irregular breathing, and pale or clammy skin. Students under stress may lose their balance from diving or being under water for a long period of time.

Anyone in charge of safety should understand the principles of hydrodynamics—how individuals move and stabilize themselves in the water. A lifeguard should be aware of how water affects the body in various situations and how the body will react. Some conditions may affect positioning and propulsion through the water; the shape, density, and stability of the swimmer also is a factor.

People with various body shapes need to be guarded differently. There are three general shapes a person's body may take—circular, rectangular, and triangular. The overweight swimmer has a circular body shape and may have difficulty finding a comfortable and safe body position. Such individuals may have problems in using their extremities for leverage and may be fearful if they are in a prone position for a long period of time. They may find their arms and legs interfere with regaining balance. People who fit into a rectangular shape, such as hemiplegics or those with unequal balance due to affected body parts, may gravitate toward the affected side. Innovative positioning must be used to obtain balance, and countermovements may have to be learned. Individuals who were swimmers before becoming disabled tend to establish a balanced position more quickly. People who have been wheelchair bound or have continually used crutches or walkers may assume the triangular position in the water. The body floats better in a V-like position, and when it is extended, the head may be submerged easily. The person may be fearful of not being able to recover; a comfortable breathing position should be found.

Proper aquatics supervision is essential for safety, and all participants should know the identity of the aquatics supervisor. All aquatics personnel should learn first aid procedures and guidelines for incidents, accidents, and emergencies in the pool, pool deck area, showers, and locker rooms. Procedures need to be practiced and updated frequently.

Good safety often means there will be no need to make a rescue. Still, circumstances are not always controllable, and knowledge and experience are necessary to effectively rescue someone in the water. Knowledge of assistive equipment and good sense about when to become involved are imperative. Also to be assessed are the nature of the condition, the number of people involved in an incident, and whether assistance will require one person or more. Sometimes a person is rescued who insists there was no need for a rescue. The lifeguard should use common sense in handling such a situation.

Volunteers

One of the greatest benefits YMCAs and other such agencies provide for their members is the opportunity to volunteer. Emphasis is placed on meeting the needs of the volunteer, who wishes to be cared about as well as given an opportunity to care. Volunteers want to grow as they help others grow, to feel they can help in the process of change, to learn as well as to help others learn, and to participate in making decisions and solving problems. They volunteer for the sociability and fun, to succeed in a team effort, and to feel they are making a difference. A volunteer deserves tangible recognition and support.

To ensure a successful volunteer program while maintaining a healthy, top-quality agency, program goals and plans must be carefully crafted. Staff supervision of volunteers should be realistic, and staff should be accessible, ready to listen, helpful, and caring.

Volunteers need guidelines. They should know the procedures and what is expected of them, and they should be involved in conferences for decision making and training along with paid staff. This can stretch "people resources." Volunteer staff should be invited to appropriate inter- and intra-agency training events and meetings; they then truly can become part of the team. When working with volunteers, use the same methods employed in measuring the performance of other personnel. Rewards and recognition should be made on a regular basis.

Common stumbling blocks in volunteer programs include the following:

- Lack of understanding of the YMCA's mission to allow every individual to realize his or her full potential
- Lack of a plan
- Lack of clear-cut staff assignments
- Tendency to resist change
- Inability to delegate important jobs to laypersons

The YMCA is an organization of volunteers. Its programs and successes both nationally and internationally depend on dedication and commitment of its volunteers. The YMCA provides a variety of opportunities for preservice and in-service training. Institutes and training sessions offer interested people a chance to gain and update skills essential in working with special populations.

Aquatics Facilities

6

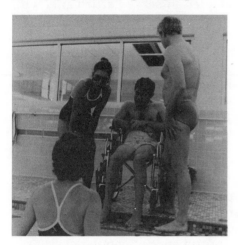

Groups with certain disabilities are often faced with physical barriers to participation in aquatics. Modifications may be necessary to adapt pools for use by these groups. Offered in this chapter are some essential guidelines for pools and suggestions for equipment that will assist the disabled to participate in aquatics.

Pool Guidelines

Very few YMCA pools have ideal facilities for those with disabilities. However, adjustments can be made inexpensively in most facilities, and while an ideal situation certainly is desirable, it is not essential.

The universal requirement for all aquatics programs is the availability of a proper water site. Many types of pools serve YMCA programs. Some are indoors, others outdoors; some are portable, others permanent. They come in myriad sizes and shapes. They may be under the ownership and control of public and private agencies, churches, hotels and motels, or even at the homes of private individuals. All pools have the potential to be used in programs for special populations, but some may require modifications. If only one pool is available, it should be a multi-use pool that can be adapted to serve participants with disabilities.

Pool temperatures should be maintained at 83 degrees and above to serve those with special needs. Air temperature should be a minimum of 2 to 5 degrees higher, depending on air circulation. Temperature requirements depend on the participants involved in the program. For example, arthritic participants need higher temperatures, based on the severity of their involvement. Those with multiple sclerosis need cooler temperatures to avoid excessive fatigue.

The pool should have extensive shallow areas. The water depth should range from 3 to 6 feet in multi-use pools. Minimum depths, particularly when lap swimming is involved, should be 3 feet on the shallow end and 6 on the deep end. A properly designed training pool can serve programs for children 5 years of age and under, older people, and special populations.

Pools must be accessible. Wide skidproof decks for safe operation of wheelchairs should be available, as should ramps, slings, hoists, and other devices for assisting individuals into and out of the water. Flotation devices also may be important, particularly for beginning swimmers.

The pool sides and bottom should be clearly marked to show depth. Lines and designs can assist in activities and in the recognition of shapes and colors. Pools designed especially for therapy fit the needs of some participants, while others do best in standard pools.

Outdoor sites, including paths, beaches, and dressing and shower facilities, also must be accessible. Shaded areas and benches may add to comfort.

Smaller pools are less costly to build and maintain than larger pools, and this should be considered when planning a new facility. All aquatics facilities should be accessible both from the parking lot and through the building. Pools should have proper lighting, nonslip surfaces, and grab bars. Wheelchair accessibility is essential in dressing rooms, locker rooms, and bathrooms as well as in the main pool area.

Remodeling a pool is sometimes impractical, and careful plans should be made to work around constraints. If the pool surface is extremely slippery, "buddies" can help disabled people out of water and around on the pool surfaces. Wide strips of indoor and outdoor carpeting can be used as "sidewalks" to and from locker rooms and pool sides. Reducing the number of swimmers in the pool may help minimize the number of collisions in the water. Additional guards or buddies can watch for swimmers who are tired and swimming in deep sections of the pool.

Equipment

Instructors differ widely on use of aquatics equipment. Some are totally opposed to flotation devices, while others will not teach beginners without them. While flotation devices are helpful in certain learning situations, students should learn to propel themselves or float without them when possible.

Flotation devices help beginners acquire skills more quickly and comfortably but should never be thought of as safety equipment. U.S. Coast Guard-approved PFDs, which may be used in some aquatics programs, should be mandatory for any boating activity and are considered safety equipment. In programs involving both nondisabled and disabled swimmers, a policy on the use of flotation devices should be established prior to beginning classes.

Some severely disabled swimmers need assistance in entering and exiting the pool. Aids that stimulate participants to take part in water activities and overcome fears and frustrations also are useful to instructors. The following lists include commercially available aids as well as those that can readily be constructed by an innovative instructor.

Equipment for Lifts, Transfers, and Support

- *Chairs/benches/shower stools*—for comfort in the pool, the pool area, and the locker room. Benches also are used as resting devices in the pool itself.
- *Flotation suit*—inflated by blowing into a valve in the front center of the suit's scoop neck. It supports a 200-pound individual. The suit can be deflated gradually when assistance no longer is needed. Some flotation suits have been taken off the market due to lack of demand.
- *Lift*—may be used for persons with temporary or permanent disabilities. The motor power of the lift should be mechanical rather than electrical, which simplifies opera-

tion and is less hazardous in the pool area. Some lifts operate on water pressure. Choice depends on need, including extent of independent entry and exit desired.

- *Neck collar*—provides neck support.
- *Pool cover*—helps preserve water temperatures at indoor and outdoor facilities. Pool covers are commercially available.
- *Pool floors*—can be any height or depth and can be designed to fit individual pools. Hydraulic platforms can be raised to deck level so wheelchairs or stretchers can be placed beside them and the swimmer can be lowered into the water.
- *Pool mat*—for assistance with transfers, exercise, and rest or as a "seizure mat" for participants following the onset of a seizure.
- *Sling*—used to assist people unable to use their arms or legs in learning aquatic skills, helps balance and support, and frees up the instructor. The canvas sling hangs from a tripod.
- *Stretcher*—can be lowered into the pool, then slipped away.
- *Transfer board*—one end placed under the student in the wheelchair, the other end on the surface of the chair to which the student is transferred with or without help.
- *Transfer Tier*^{tm}—steps with handrails that can be submerged in the pool.
- *Wheelchair*—works well in aquatic areas if shower chair or stainless steel chair.

Transfers should be done only by experienced personnel.

Easy Ladder^{tm}
(Photograph courtesy of Triad Technologies, Inc.)

Transfer Tier*tm*
(Photograph courtesy of Triad Technologies, Inc.)

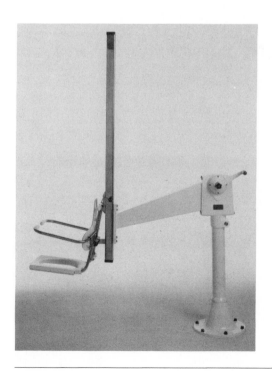

Aquanaids lift
(Photograph courtesy of William M. Smith and Associates, Inc.)

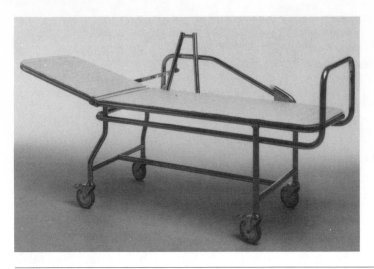

Wheeled chair for Aquanaids lift
(Photograph courtesy of William M. Smith and Associates, Inc.)

Hoyer swimming pool lifter
(Photograph courtesy of Ted Hoyer and Company, Inc.)

Teaching Equipment

- Ankle-wrist flotation devices
- Barbells
- Diving rings
- Floating balls
- Frisbees
- Hula-hoops, weighted and unweighted
- Kickboards
- Kick rollers
- Mask, fins, and snorkles
- Parallel bars
- Plinths-aquatic teaching platforms
- Seats
- Swim goggles
- Toys and game equipment

In addition, washcloths, towels, bleach bottles or milk bottles, ropes, inner tubes, Ping-Pong balls, and other objects may be useful as teaching aids and for various games. Toys should be used under close supervision, especially ropes, which participants may find helpful in moving themselves through the water, and inner tubes.

Special Populations

7

To work with special populations, program developers and instructors should learn as much as possible about the various disabilities. As a beginning, many different categories of disability and their common affects on individuals are listed in this chapter. In some cases there are also tips on how to compensate for or avoid problems the disability might cause. However, this is only an introduction to each type of disability; more information should be sought before beginning any program. The bibliography in appendix B lists many good sources for such information.

Two terms that are often used when discussing special populations are *impaired* and *disabled*. There are some important differences between them. *Impaired persons* have identifiable organic or functional conditions. Part of the body may be missing, or one or more parts of the body may not be functioning adequately. The condition may be permanent, as in the case of amputations, congenital birth defects, cerebral palsy, and brain damage, or it may be temporary, as in functional speech defects, some learning disabilities, various emotional problems, certain social maladjustments, and specific movement deficiencies. Postsurgical conditions and illnesses or accidental injuries may cause temporary impairments. *Disabled persons* are limited or restricted in performing some skills and in doing specific jobs, tasks, or activities because of impairments. Some impaired persons attain levels of excellence in activities they are considered unable to perform. Congenital quadriamputees have learned to swim and dive; people disabled by polio, paraplegics, and individuals with cerebral palsy have become competitive swimmers; and many others have participated in waterskiing, kayaking, and other water activities. Other terms related to special populations are listed in the glossary.

The emphasis in placing people in aquatics programs should be on functional ability. Individuals who can take part in mainstream activities safely, successfully, and comfortably should be encourged to do so. When confidence, skill, emotional stability, overall control, or some other vital element is lacking, people may do better by beginning in partially mainstreamed programs. Those with severe, profound, or multiple disabilities may need the special opportunities and experiences available in segregated programs.

In all cases, the manner in which a program is adapted will depend on the individuals involved. Each person will have a unique set of abilities, depending on the severity of the disability, the progression of the condition, and individual strengths and weaknesses. Although some common characteristics of populations are listed in this chapter, instructors must judge each situation individually.

Alzheimer's Disease

Alzheimer's disease afflicts about 7 percent of the over-65 population, killing the victim in two ways. First the mind dies, along with its essential core of recent and long-past memories. Names of loved ones may be forgotten; dates, places, and skills fade from recognition. Tying a shoelace, cutting food, and reading a clock may become insurmountable tasks. Next, the body dies. Those with Alzheimer's may be unable to walk or control bodily functions. Gradually the person sinks into a coma and never regains consciousness or dies of other complications, such as pneumonia.

Some of those who suffer from Alzheimer's disease may be ill for as long as 20 years, particularly those who acquire the disease at relatively young ages, in their 50s or 60s. The average length of decline is about 7 years. Alzheimer's disease is irreversible, striking every ethnic and socioeconomic group. As people live longer, the numbers grow. It is the fourth leading cause of death among older people; only heart disease, cancer, and stroke claim more victims. It also accounts for more than half the cases of senile dementia in the United States.

Clumps of twisted nerve-cell fibers are characteristic of the disorder. But these "neurofibrillary tangles" are present in the brains of people who never had Alzheimer's as well. Small strokes that knock out increasingly large amounts of brain tissue may mimic Alzheimer's disease, as may other conditions such as depression, thyroid disease, vitamin deficiency, alcoholism, drug reaction, and anemia. Since many of these conditions are reversible, it is essential to get a correct diagnosis when Alzheimer-like symptoms strike.

Normal age-related forgetfulness is not Alzheimer's. Misplacing a notebook or forgetting the name of an acquaintance are consistent with good health. When work or social life become affected, the matter may be more serious. Other Alzheimer's symptoms include trouble with language, personality change, inability to follow words on a page, and apraxia (difficulty in performing rote gestures such as brushing teeth or wiping crumbs off a table). In a later stage, the person may act inappropriately. Next comes incontinence, forgetting the season, and forgetting names of children or spouse. Some patients become agitated and sociopathic, threatening the safety and well-being of others. The ability to talk disappers, as does the ability to walk.

Familes who care for a parent or relative with Alzheimer's disease often become physically, emotionally, and financially drained. Therapeutic and recreational programs for the afflicted person, such as aquatics, give the caretaker some respite.

Amputees

Whether the cause is congenital, accidental, or surgical, all amputees basically experience the same physical effects in water. Since they have less body weight, their buoyancy is better. Although their sense of balance in floating and swimming positions may be affected, most lower limb single or double amputees can learn to swim readily. Amputations above the knee usually do affect balance and buoyancy. Depending on the amount of stump on a person, flippers can be attached and can

add significantly to propulsion. Arm amputations may adverse-
ly affect buoyancy and balance in floating; small flippers can be
attached to these stumps, which is especially useful when swimming on the back. When body weight is unbalanced because of
an amputation, weight can be equalized by bending the remaining leg to accommodate weight loss or lowering the remaining
arm to the side to give a cross balance of weights.

For students with hemiplegia—a condition involving total or
partial paralysis of one side of the body—the initial step is learning to maintain balance in the water.

The paraplegic—with partial or complete paralysis of the
lower half of the body—may become a very good swimmer. The
suggested sequence for teaching the paraplegic is establishing
balance, teaching the float, and adding arm movements on the
back. A breaststroke, overarm stroke, and crawl can be done in
the prone position. Safety procedures should be stressed.

The triplegic—with partial or complete paralysis affecting
three limbs—requires some trial and error and patience. Starting on the back and using a regular sequence may work well,
and the instructor should make certain that the student can
breathe and turn from back to front and front to back. Flotation
devices can be very helpful in adjusting, balancing, and gaining
momentum.

The quadriplegic—with partial or complete paralysis of all
four limbs—can begin by learning to float using flotation devices.
Flippers on the student's stumps can be helpful. (See the University of Texas film "Quad Amputee," listed in appendix A.) A
newly designed sling that enables instructors to work on movement also is available now. Mat work in the gym or at home is
useful in learning to turn over. Teaching participants to breathe
while turning from the back to the front and to the back again
may take some time and may not be an instruction priority.

Students whose amputations were necessitated because of
diabetes should cover the stump with a sock to protect it from
abrasion. Socks or stockings may be used with many paraplegics
and quadriplegics and some spina bifida participants. Caution
must be taken with anyone who has problems with peripheral
circulation, feels no pain when injured, or has difficulty healing.

Psychological and social maladjustments are not unusual in
people with one or more limbs missing, and often problems arise
from attitudes of others. Students who recently have experienced
the loss of a limb may still be in the process of grief and acceptance. A matter-of-fact, direct approach, empathetic rather than
sympathetic, works well.

Aphasia

Aphasia is a symptom generally associated with cerebral pathology and may be the result of a cerebral vascular accident—an injury or stroke. It is an inability to appropriately formulate words in an intelligent manner. Some people with aphasia cannot speak at all, and while they understand what is being said, they cannot respond in an appropriate manner. Each person must be assessed individually.

When a person cannot comprehend or has difficulty comprehending language, that person is said to have receptive aphasia. If someone cannot find the correct word to express an idea or communicate verbally, that person is said to have expressive aphasia. Both types of aphasia can occur in the same person, who may or may not know such a problem exists.

Speech disabilities can result from severe social deprivation or a physical disability such as cerebral palsy. Mental retardation and severe emotional disturbance also can cause disability in speech, as can a severe hearing impairment or deafness.

Arthritis and Related Disorders

Arthritis includes many disorders. Each arthritic participant should be treated on an individual basis in cooperation with a physician. The Arthritis Foundation and the YMCA have established an aquatics program for people with arthritis; a manual for that program is available through the YMCA Program Store.

A few general rules will help the instructor: Water should be as warm as possible, and the participant should exercise moderately. Fatigue, soreness, and discomfort after an aquatics session may worsen the condition.

Three types of arthritis commonly seen in aquatics programs are osteoarthritis, rheumatoid arthritis, and Still's disease (juvenile rheumatoid arthritis). Osteoarthritis is the most common form of arthritis; many older people are affected to some degree. Symptoms include weakness and muscle spasms around a joint, fatigue, pain, deformity, and joints so unstable they may "give out."

Osteoarthritis is the wearing out of a joint, caused by a disturbance in the mechanics of the joint leading to uneven distribution of weight on the joint's surfaces. The joints may be abnormally strained because of daily activities or occupational hazards. Dockworkers may have osteoarthritis in their backs; assembly workers may have it in their fingers. The most commonly affected joints are those in the back, the hips, and the knees—all weight-bearing joints subjected to hard work. Flare-ups and remissions of the pain are common. Heat and analgesic drugs provide some relief from pain and inflammation.

Rheumatoid arthritis is a chronic systemic disease. Joints become inflamed and bones thin, atrophied, and misshapen. In the early stages, the disease manifests itself as a migratory stiffness and swelling in various joints of the body. Deformities typify later stages. The cause is unknown, and there is no cure. The disease affects more women than men but strikes adults of all ages. Often it worsens progressively. Pain may be relieved through physical therapy, application of heat, medications, joint replacement surgery, and even acupuncture and biofeedback.

Still's disease has the same symptoms as adult rheumatoid arthritis with the addition of enlargement of the lymph nodes, liver, and spleen. It may lead to impairment of growth and development, and the victim may remain short, have short limbs and small digits, or have an underdeveloped lower jaw with a receding chin. Still's disease often subsides when puberty begins. Prognosis for recovery is more favorable than in the adult form of arthritis. Physical therapy and proper exercise are particularly important in reducing contractures and restoring strength to weak muscle groups.

Asthma

Asthma is a common medical disorder, often caused by an allergic reaction to something in the environment, food, or strenuous exercise. Water activity often is beneficial for the asthmatic person. However, if a symptom-free participant develops asthmatic symptoms in the pool, he or she should be taken out of the environment immediately. Many different irritating substances, including pollen, dust, or chlorine, may be responsible for the condition.

An asthmatic person responds to certain irritating substances with symptoms such as tightness in the chest and wheezing that leads to shortness of breath. Wheezing and shortness of breath result from constriction of air passages. The asthmatic then is unable to take in air and expel it properly. If untreated, respiratory paralysis and even death may occur. Medications tend to neutralize the bronchial spasm and open up air passages to permit normal breathing. Underwater swimming and diving and other forced attempts at holding the breath may need to be avoided.

Childhood asthma often may be outgrown. Asthma is described sometimes as the "vulnerable child syndrome," since breathing attacks frighten the child and parents, and parents may become overprotective.

Stress may be a factor in bringing on asthma. Instructors should emphasize the adjustment process, breathing, and breath control. The participant should be physically prepared to handle the challenges of the program. Exercise also can be therapeutic.

Autism

Autism is the inability to respond to external stimuli such as sounds, smells, commands, and pictures. Autistic people may appear to be mute, since they have no apparent recognition of stimuli. When a child under 30 months of age manifests a profound and general failure to develop social relationships, is retarded in speaking and comprehending, echoes words or phrases, speaks of himself or herself in the second or third person, and is very ritualistic and compulsive in behavior, the child has early infantile autism. Males are more likely to be affected. Often autistic children have parents who are highly intelligent and unusual achievers. Convincing evidence exists that autism may be the result of central nervous system impairments, prenatal damage, or perinatal damage.

Usually present from the beginning of life, autism requires a combined, supportive treatment program. Medications may be given to decrease anxiety and reactions of rage. Behavior modification may be helpful in decreasing socially unacceptable and self-injurious behavior. If oral communication is impossible, sign language or other ways to communicate may work. With proper support, many families raise autistic children at home. Usually the autistic child has a worse prognosis than the mentally retarded child with the same IQ. Few ever function effectively in society or hold jobs, and the majority eventually are institutionalized.

Since many autistic people have good gross motor and visual-perceptual skills, instructional programs can be developed around these abilities. Stimulating activities including such programs as aquatics help the autistic individual develop to his or her full potential. A variety of teaching methods should be used, depending on the severity of the autism and the particular individual affected. Instructors should work on a prescription teaching basis and contact community resources for assistance.

Brain Damage

Brain damage often results from an injury, trauma, or illness. Causes range from cardiopulmonary arrest to inborn errors of metabolism, infection, stroke, seizure disorder, or any accident involving the head. When a child suffers a head injury that affects intelligence during the developmental years, the child may be classified as retarded. The same injury in adults puts them in the category of being brain damaged.

Brain damage means that a certain area of the brain has been injured, but it does not necessarily result in retardation. In some cases the condition can be reversible, can be compensated for through education and relearning, or can be reflected as a physical disability rather than a mental one.

Brain-injured syndrome includes the following behaviors: difficulties in perception, very high activity levels, distractibility and poor attention span, impulsive behavior, and emotional instability. Neuromotor system defects also may be present. Health disorders resulting from brain damage, such as cerebral palsy, cannot be cured, but physical therapy and sometimes surgery can improve function. Teaching techniques and special programming should be constructed to meet individual needs.

Brittle Bones

Brittle bones, or osteogenesis imperfecta, is a condition caused by demineralization of the bone and is characterized by bone fragility. Afflicted individuals must be protected as much as possible from bumps and bruises. In aquatics, instructors should not allow these participants to jump, dive, or bump each other. Contact with hard surfaces can be avoided by working in the center of the pool. If the participant complains of pain, the activity should immediately be terminated. If any problem arises, an appropriate person—parent, guardian, teacher, or physician—should be contacted at once and an incident report should be prepared and filed.

Cancer

Cancer is unrestricted new cell growth anywhere in the body that tends to spread and destroy tissue. Not all tumors are solid; various types of cancer proliferate in the blood or marrow. Aside from the physical malaise accompanying both cancer and the radical treatments used to combat the spread of the disease, cancer patients may experience psychological and emotional turmoil. Even victims who undergo successful treatment will not know for approximately 5 years whether or not they are "cured."

Cancer strikes people of all ages, both sexes, and all races, ethnic groups, and socioeconomic levels. Some forms are relatively mild, others almost always fatal. Early detection and healthy life-styles—including good nutrition, no smoking, and regular exercise—probably play a part in preventing cancer. Heredity, too, has a role in who will eventually develop the disease. Constant research into better treatment and prevention is moving medicine toward effectively combating the disease.

There are numerous forms of cancer, and programs should be developed on an individual basis. Participants in aquatics currently may be under treatment for cancer. They already may have had some form of surgery to stop its spread or may be undergoing radiation or chemotherapy. Physical therapy, including aquatics, may help them on their way to recovery or may help ease pain, reestablish a positive feeling about self-image, restore confidence, or fight depression. Many mastectomy patients participate in aquatics. Water experiences increase their muscle strength and provide a good avenue for fitness and socialization. Special activities and water exercises have been developed for mastectomy patients. Many participate in regular swimming programs. A local mastectomy support group or cancer organization should be contacted for further information.

Cardiac Disease

Congenital heart disease, particularly in children, may be worsened by a change in activity level. Older persons with valvular heart or coronary artery disease also must be cautious not to strain their hearts. Tolerance for exercise can slowly be established and intensity of action as well as duration of the exercise increased progressively. The activity limits prescribed by a physician should never be exceeded. The physician can update the prescription as the patient becomes stronger. Ideally, cardiac evaluations can be done frequently if a person is doing well within the program, which involves the physician more closely in the program.

Instructors and volunteers who work with heart patients should be thoroughly trained in cardiopulmonary resuscitation (CPR). Emergency numbers for medical assistance and hospital transportation should be close at hand. Any sign of chest pain, shortness of breath, cyanosis (a bluish color possibly indicating a decrease of oxygen content in the blood), or undue fatigue calls for immediate medical evaluation. The program's medical advisory committee should outline procedures to follow.

Before participants begin an aquatics class, they should be asked about their general well-being. Lack of sleep, emotional problems, medications, and a variety of other factors may influence cardiac problems. The activity level for the day can be designed keeping these stress-related details in mind.

Instructors should know how to take a pulse. A normal pulse rate before exercise followed by a rate that is too elevated afterward may be cause for alarm. The student's physician should be called if the pulse is irregular. If the class is part of a rehabilitation program, having a physician or nurse on hand might be beneficial. Occasionally a class member may have cardiac disease without knowing it. If chest pains or shortness of breath develops, the participant should be evaluated by trained personnel. Cyanosis also may be dangerous and symptomatic of an underlying heart condition.

Cerebral Palsy

The term *cerebral palsy* describes a condition caused by damage to the brain during the prenatal, natal, or postnatal period. Cerebral palsy is characterized by lesions in the central nervous system that produce motor, sensory, emotional, and intellectual impairments. However, it does not necessarily have these manifestations. Many people with cerebral palsy have high intellectual capabilities.

The four main types of cerebral palsy are as follows:

- Spastic—certain muscles tend to show reflex action. When the muscles are to be moved, they contract and prevent the intended movement, causing muscle stiffness.
- Athetoid—excessive movement and tension when movements are resisted. The individual with this type of cerebral palsy seems to squirm constantly. Affected parts of the body wriggle despite valiant attempts to control them.
- Ataxia—lack of balance and coordination, a tendency to fall. The person may stagger in walking but is not in constant motion and is not paralyzed. The individual is quiet and appears unaffected, except when making certain motions.
- Rigid—muscles that are stiff but not tense.

Cerebral palsy has many variations. Some people may experience multiple problems such as seizure and speech impairment. The instructor should learn about each student's specific disability. The time needed for learning a skill or adjusting to water may be shortened if parents or others work with the student in a bathtub or whirlpool. The participant also can help by offering suggestions.

Students should be urged to go into deep water as soon as possible, as it affords better support and makes it easier to move. The instructor must be able to stand in the water, but the student need not. Independence should be encouraged.

Students can adjust to the water environment through aquatics play activities and patience and understanding from the instructor. Seeing peers perform skills may encourage and motivate them. Demonstrating how a relaxed muscle feels may help the participant learn to relax. Each lesson should end on a note of success.

Cerebral-Vascular Accident

A cerebral-vascular accident—stroke or apoplexy—is caused by a rupture and the resulting hemorrhage or thrombus (clot) in one of the cerebral arteries. Hemiplegic paralysis—paralysis of one side of the body—is immediately apparent on the side opposite the lesion, and the face is affected on the same side as the lesion. Difficulty with speech or understanding language points to a lesion in the dominant half of the cerebral cortex. For the majority of people, those who are right-handed, this will be the left half of the brain, the section that contains areas of speech, hearing, and analytical task solving.

Treatment for preventing physical helplessness and deformity should start during the acute period. Deformities that follow a cerebal-vascular accident are basically the same, no matter the cause or extent of the lesion. At the onset, the paralysis is most often flaccid in both the upper and lower extremities on the affected side. Some extremities may become spastic, or one extremity may become spastic while the other remains flaccid.

Aquatics helps by providing direct stimulation and encouraging communication. Some students who have suffered strokes may have difficulty understanding, so short sentences and simple instructions are best. Responses may come in the form of bizarre, inaccurate use of language and swearing. Instructors should help to provide correct language.

Diabetes

Diabetes is a condition in which the body's pancreas is unable to produce sufficient insulin, which is necessary to utilize the excess sugar in the blood. The diabetic consequently has an excess of sugar in the blood that can lead to many complications, such as acceleration of hardening of the arteries leading to vascular disease, kidney disease, and blindness. This affliction is treated with a proper diabetic diet, an exercise program that aids in reducing excess weight, and, in severe cases, insulin to lower the excess blood sugar.

Diabetes is one of the three major diseases that kill, after heart disease and cancer. If afflicts millions of Americans. There are two types of diabetes: the first usually has its onset in childhood or young adulthood and requires lifelong treatment. Its warning signs are frequent urination, unusual thirst, rapid weight loss, fatigue, nausea, and extreme hunger. The majority of diabetics have the second type, which most frequently strikes people over 40. Its warning signs may include those of the first type as well as excessive weight, blurred vision or a change in vision, tingling or numbness in the feet or legs, frequent skin rashes or infections, and slow healing of cuts and bruises. This type of diabetes often can be managed by a diet that reduces blood sugar levels, exercise that helps decrease excess sugar levels and weight, and medication.

Aquatics instructors should be aware that class participants may be taking insulin either orally or by injection and may be subject to insulin shock brought on by exercise, an overdose of insulin, or too little food. Too much sugar in the blood and not enough insulin may result in a diabetic coma. Diabetics should wear medic alert tags.

Symptoms of insulin shock include breathing deeply, sighing, and having dry and flushed skin. Breath may have an acetone odor. The instructor should know when the student last ate and last took medication.

Since diabetics are slow to heal, the instructor should take precautions to see that they avoid skin abrasion and bruising. Students can wear socks to protect their feet.

Dyslexia

The term *dyslexia* literally means poor or inadequate verbal language. Dyslexic people learn language more slowly than others and may not use language effectively. However, they are neither brain damaged nor retarded and may, in fact, be extremely intelligent. Albert Einstein was dyslexic. More males seem to have dyslexia than females.

Dyslexic students may need more repetition of material; the learning process is gradual and slow. Dyslexia is a learning disability that often causes problems in reading and writing. A learning disabled person is often very frustrated and has a poor self-image.

Activities that bring success help build confidence. Success in aquatics is very important to someone with a learning disability, and instructors should be supportive and encouraging. Exercises and games that establish left-right movement help the dyslexic student learn swimming skills. Touching and hearing also can reinforce learning. Programs should be geared toward the individual participant, who should learn one skill well before going on to the next skill.

Epilepsy

The term *epilepsy* applies to any disorder in which convulsions or seizures are present. Epilepsy is a disturbance in the electrochemical activity of the brain. It may be a syptom of an underlying disease, such as a tumor growing in or near the motor areas of the brain or irritation caused by inflammation, or it may follow a head injury. With proper treatment and medication, 80 percent of epileptics are almost totally free of symptoms. Many people who are subject to seizures function well in all phases of life.

The four common types of seizures are as follows:

- Grand mal—occurs at any age and may be associated with organic brain disease. An aura, a sensation of light, or disorientation may warn the epileptic of an oncoming attack. Convulsions are preceded by unconsciousness.

- Petit mal—occurs mainly in childhood and consists of momentary loss of consciousness, staring into space, and blinking without focusing.

- Psychomotor—may develop at any age and is characterized by uncontrolled body movements such as twitching and confusion. It often is associated with organic brain injury.

- Jacksonian—caused by tumors, inflammation, injury, or hemorrhage and characterized by convulsions on one side of the body.

If an individual has multiple seizures, a seizure that lasts more than 5 minutes, or a history of hospitalization, he or she should be taken to a hospital.

People with epilepsy may participate in aquatics programs. The instructor and others in charge should be aware of the disorder and should check with the epileptic or his or her family that the prescribed medication has been taken. They also should know what to do in case of a seizure. Students can wear a brightly colored bathing cap or suit for quick identification in case of seizure; this should be left to their discretion.

Most seizures can be treated simply. If it takes place on deck, the individual should be placed on a mat away from obstacles. Tight clothing should be loosened and a soft object such as a piece of clothing, a towel, or a pillow put beneath the head to keep the person's airway open. After the convulsion, the individual should be rolled on his or her side to allow secretions to drain from the nose and mouth. Nothing should be placed in the person's mouth during a seizure.

If the seizure takes place in the pool, the student should be taken to the shallow water, away from the edge. The airway should be kept open and the seizure finished in the water. If the seizure lasts more than a minute or is repeated or medical records show that the individual should always be hospitalized after a seizure, then he or she should be taken to the hospital. Certified personnel should help remove the epileptic from the water if hospitalization is necessary. Otherwise, after the seizure the instructor should take the student to a place outside of the pool where he or she can rest. It may be best not to permit any more aquatics that day.

Overexertion, fatigue, anxiety, and fear can bring on seizures. Students should have time to rest during each class.

Hemophilia

Hemophilia is a hereditary condition in which the blood fails to clot quickly enough, causing prolonged, uncontrollable bleeding from even a small cut, a bruise, or overexertion. Hemophilia involves the muscular and subcutaneous tissues of joints and every organ in the body.

Hemophiliac aquatics participants should be well protected from any trauma or injury, such as striking their elbows when climbing out of the pool or excessively propelling their legs. A blow on the head, chest, or abdomen can lead to serious internal bleeding and even death.

Instructors should teach skills slowly and gently, determining the effect of kicking and other body movements. The degree of hemophilia is variable; some participants may tolerate a great deal of exercise while others will show signs of bleeding and hemorrhaging with a minimum amount of exercise. If any bleeding is noticed, the hemophiliac should be referred at once to a physician or the emergency room of the nearest hospital. Serious bleeding may be hidden behind what appears as just a superficial bruise.

An individualized or small group program in which likelihood of injury is lessened may be best suited to the hemophiliac.

Hydrocephalus

Hydrocephalus is created by a blockage in the brain's ventricular system and results in an obstruction of the normal circulation of cerebral spinal fluid. Because the spinal fluid cannot drain normally, brain tissue is destroyed. The hydrocephalic usually is pictured in the advanced stage with an abnormal enlargement of the head, which creates the illusion of a small face and protruding forehead. Some hydrocephalics are normal or even superior in intelligence; some are mentally retarded to some degree.

In most cases, inserting one or more specialized tubes, called *shunts*, is necessary. The shunt is placed in the ventrical of the brain, which has expanded under cerebral spinal pressure. The spinal liquid may be shunted through the jugular vein, the plural cavity, or the abdominal cavity. The bypass of the obstructed ventricular system decreases the ventricular pressure, which decreases brain destruction. By decreasing brain pressure, normal head size is usually maintained.

Learning Disabilities

Learning disabilities usually are disorders of the central nervous system that interfere with one or more basic learning functions, such as collecting, sorting, storing, or expressing information. Some learning disabilities are mild and can be overcome alone; others require extensive, individualized assistance. People who have learning disabilities often can be mainstreamed.

Some experts believe learning disabilities are caused by illness or injury during pregnancy, birth, or shortly after birth. Others believe they have a hereditary cause. Learning disabilities are not caused by defects in sensory organs, emotional problems, mental retardation, or cultural deprivation. Many are discovered when school problems occur. They may affect speaking, listening, reading, writing, or numerical calculation and may overlap. Immediate individualized programming is important.

Most learning disabled people can become achievers. They may be successful in a variety of fields, from business to the arts. Some are exceptionally creative and are imaginative problem solvers, such as doctors, scientists, or inventors.

The learning disabled individual can succeed in aquatics, but the instructor is the key. Each successfully learned skill provides a base on which to learn a new one. Aquatics is fun and can be carried over to leisure time and educational pursuits, but discipline also should be maintained, and there should be a consistent daily class routine. An individualized program plan is important, and the instructor should frequently review program notes with participants.

Mental Illness

More people are incapacitated by mental illness than by all other health problems combined. Recreation is of significant value to the mentally disturbed, and aquatics are effective for working with those who are hard to reach. Through aquatics the mentally ill person can better blend into society, learn to care for himself or herself, feel part of a group, communicate freely, and build self-confidence. Aquatics also help participants relax and learn to trust people. Successful experiences in aquatics may aid in establishing patterns of social adjustment.

People with personality disorders need very structured programs with many specific objectives. Routine is important. By establishing rules, setting limitations, and imposing time factors, aggression, hostility, and other unacceptable behaviors can be controlled and channeled into healthy outlets. Impulsive behavior can be channeled into spontaneous activity. The instructor should spend time in the water with each individual, and the approach should be based on building success experiences.

The disturbed individual frequently is impulsive, disorganized, aggressive, and negative. The instructor's interest in the person should be positive without deep emotional involvement. An abundance of patience, diplomacy, and calmness is needed. Praise helps build confidence; progressions may be slow, but each skill learned should receive special attention.

Some mentally ill people are "touch sensitive"; they are very reluctant to have any direct physical contact. The instructor should use good judgment in approaching these students. Friendly but cautious overtures may work well.

Bizarre behavior patterns—profanity, nudity, masturbation, noises, aggressive movements, and threatening gestures—are part of the normal pool environment with this population. The instructor should check with those who normally work with the students to find the best way to deal with such problems.

Mental Retardation

Mental retardation may be present at birth or caused by brain damage acquired as the result of illness, accident, or deprivation. Mentally retarded people have the potential for exhibiting the same range of abilities as the nonretarded in performing physical and motor activities. The mentally retarded child may appear perfectly normal, and people around him or her may have normal expectations that the child cannot fulfill. Frustration may result.

Down's syndrome, caused by an extra chromosome, is characterized by a combination of unique physical features associated with mental retardation. It is easily recognized at an early age. People with Down's syndrome are usually friendly, pleasant, and nonaggressive, but they can be quite stubborn. Up to 10 percent of people with Down's syndrome suffer from atlantoxial dislocation, a malalignment of the cervical vertebrae that exposes them to the possibility of injury or paralysis if they hyperextend or radically flex the neck muscles. Aquatics activities such as diving, the butterfly stroke, starts, and turns should be avoided, as should any other activity that puts pressure on the head and neck muscles. Incidence of an injury occurring, however, is rare. The Special Olympics has had no injuries related to this condition in its 18-year history. Down's syndrome people often excel in aquatics.

A malfunction of the thyroid gland causes a condition known as cretinism. Glandular treatments given shortly after birth can prevent the condition, but if treatment is delayed, the condition becomes permanent. People with this condition are usually docile, pleasant, and friendly.

A rare type of mental disburbance, phenylketonuria (PKU), is a metabolic disturbance in which the body cannot convert the substance phenylalanine, found in protein. The toxic substance circulating through the body damages the brain cells. PKU's manifestations are severe retardation sometimes accompanied by a complete lack of speech, overactivity, aggression, and distractibility and hard-to-manage behavior. A simple test given immediately after birth will show if the condition is present. A special diet started 2 weeks after birth gives the child a good chance to develop normally.

Other types of mental retardation distinguised by physical characteristics include microcephaly (extremely small head), in which the brain is compressed because of small skull capacity; macrocephaly (large head); and hydrocephaly (water on the brain).

Multiple Sclerosis

Multiple sclerosis is one of the most common organic diseases affecting the nervous system and chiefly attacks the brain and spinal cord. Rarely fatal in its early stages, it may be progressive and cause long incapacity. It usually involves many parts of the nervous system and is characterized by relapses followed by periods of partial and sometimes complete remission.

Symptoms may include periods of partial to complete paralysis of the legs, trunk, and arms. With or without paralysis, those with multiple sclerosis may suffer lack of coordination with staggering and tremor or poor coordination with tremors of the extremities and sometimes of the body and head. Numbness, tingling, and various sensory changes also may occur. Eye symptoms are common and include involuntary movement of the eyeball, periods of double or blurred vision, and temporary to permanent blindness in one or both eyes. In advanced cases those afflicted may experience slurred speech and sometimes difficulty with bladder and bowel control.

Physical therapy can relieve spasticity, increase coordination, and help the individual learn to substitute nonaffected muscles for impaired ones. Muscular therapy, except in acute phases, is important.

Students with multiple sclerosis should be programmed individually. Their lessons should begin slowly, going from 10 minutes per session to the maximum that is beneficial. Cheerfulness helps to counteract a tendency toward depression that is common of people with multiple sclerosis. Encouragement can be useful, but instructors should dissuade participants from trying to do everything the way they used to.

Water that is warmer than normal pool temperature may be fatiguing for these students. Locker room assistance should be available. If a wheelchair and lift are involved, students should understand how they will be assisted to and from the pool. Some students may find flotation devices useful in the water.

Muscular Dystrophy

Muscular dystrophy, a chronic disease of the muscles, often begins in early childhood. A gradual weakening of the muscles takes place as muscle tissue is progressively replaced with fat tissue over the years. As the disease progresses, the victim becomes confined to a wheelchair and eventually to bed.

The six clinical types of muscular dystrophy are these:

- Duchenne's disease—occurs almost exclusively in males between the ages of 1 to 6. Victims have a poor prognosis, as many die before the age of 20. It often is accompanied by mental retardation. Lordosis, characterized by a waddling gait, distinguishes this form of the condition.

- Becker's dystrophy—involves the pelvofemoral musculature and is relatively benign.

- Leyden-Mobius—involves the shoulder and pelvic girdle, usually beginning in preadolescence.

- Facio-scapulo-humeral dystrophy—has a slow but variable progression. Victims have a virtually normal life expectancy.

- Myotonic dystrophy—slowly involves the chewing and swallowing muscles. It is often accompanied by mental retardation.

- Ophthalmoplegic dystrophy—attacks the eye muscles and progresses to the face and neck.

All types are hereditary. When muscular dystrophy begins in adult life, the prognosis is good. Usually only the facial, neck, and shoulder muscles are involved. When muscular dystrophy is fatal, death is usually due to complications brought on by other illnesses that the weakened muscles are unable to combat.

Swimming provides an opportunity for those with muscular dystrophy to retain as much functioning as possible and to possibly alleviate feelings of depression and hopelessness. Because people with muscular dystrophy have a great deal of fat tissue, they float easily despite the often flexed contractures of their limbs. Their arms and legs, restricted in movement outside of the water, can move easily in the pool. Swimming offers an outlet for physical needs that otherwise cannot be met. Muscular dystrophy students do not have control of their heads, so they need a floating headrest or careful surveillance. The back position works best in the pool, and children may work well with assistance from their parents.

The elementary backstroke can be taught to muscular dystrophy students from the backfloat position with little difficulty. A modified frog or flutter kick usually is used. Jumping or falling into the water from very low heights is permitted but not encouraged. Inner tubes should never be used; the student can be in danger of slipping through the tube or flipping forward.

Games and simple activities should stress enjoyment and range of motion in all movements, and care should be taken that students are not beyond their limits. When lifting an individual with muscular dystrophy, the instructor should not depend on the shoulder girdle, which may have no strength, but should hold onto the bathing suit.

Orthopedic Impairments and Disabilities

Orthopedically disabled people, those with skeletal or muscular abnormalities, may have slower, less free motor functions as well as poor balance. Movement often is inefficient, and fatigue may be a concern; but the specific impairment may be less of a problem than are poor self-image and lack of socialization.

The different types of orthopedic disabilities are as follows:

- One lower extremity involved, such as an amputation.
- Hemiplegia—upper and lower extremities on the same side of the body involved. The affected side may be spastic or flaccid.
- Paraplegia—both lower extremities as well as trunk involved. The impaired parts may be spastic or flaccid.
- Quadriplegia—all four extremities as well as trunk involved. The affected parts may be spastic or flaccid.

Water is the only environment in which seriously impaired people can be completely independent. Sometimes distorted movements are so improved in the water that an instructor may have difficulty determining which students have orthopedic impairments.

Beginning swimmers with impaired leg movements need the security of being able to right their bodies and stand. Classes should include careful and patient instruction in treading water and floating. Students with flaccid paralysis of limbs usually float easily, since their limbs are buoyant.

Students who have lost the use of an arm may be better at asymmetrical strokes, such as the modified sidestroke, the single overarm stroke, and the trudgeon stroke. Those who have the use of one leg may be best at symmetrical strokes on the back or stomach, such as the elementary backstroke, the breaststroke, and the back- and frontcrawl. If both arms or legs are severely affected, symmetrical strokes provide the best balance. For students with an affected arm and leg on the same side of the body, symmetrical strokes are easiest.

A student whose leg and thigh muscles are very weak generally can use a modified scissors kick rather than a whip kick. People with severe back or abdominal weakness, such as those who have had polio, do better in a prone or supine position rather than lying on their side.

Osteoporosis

In osteoporosis, bone mass is slowly reabsorbed by the body. The bone that remains becomes fragile and susceptible to fracture. Twenty million people nationwide have osteoporosis; it accounts for 13 million fractures annually. Abnormal porousness of the bones also may contribute to a variety of ailments, from backache to dowager's hump. Decalcification and weakening of the bony structure often lead to fractures, and when this affects the spine, it can cause much pain.

Osteoporosis has been linked to hormone deficiencies that accompany the aging process as well as to the slowing down of bone-cell replacement by the body. Thin, white women are particularly at risk for osteoporosis.

To avoid or reverse osteoporosis, people need to do weight-bearing exercise regularly. Even modest increases in exercise, such as walking, will help. Daily exercise strengthens bones and adds new bone mass to make up for mass reabsorbed by the body. In addition, people should include calcium-rich foods in their diet. Those over 40 should consume about 1,500 milligrams of calcium every day. Milk products are by far the best source of calcium. However, some adults, especially those of Asian,

Mediterranean, or African descent, cannot digest the lactose found in milk sugar. Enzymes that aid in the digestion of milk are available at pharmacies. Tofu, a curd made from soybeans, also is rich in calcium. People who require calcium supplements should also get a vitamin D supplement. A good source of natural vitamin D is sunshine.

Instructors should treat students with osteoporosis with extra care because their bones are brittle. Students should enter and exit the pool carefully.

Parkinson's Disease

Parkinson's disease, a disease with a very slow onset, is characterized by slowness and rigidity of movement. It is caused by the malfunction of a specialized part of the brain associated with voluntary movement and is more frequent in men than in women. The onset usually occurs between ages 50 and 65 and may not be noticed.

Symptoms include a shuffling walk that often breaks into a run, rigidity of the arm muscles, a "pill rolling" tremor in the hands, and a mask-like, expressionless quality in the face. The affected person has little control over movement and cannot begin walking or, once going, has trouble stopping. Rigidity of the muscles causes fatigue and pain. If the throat muscles are involved, speech is slow and slurred. Voluntary movements take so long to begin that reactions seem very slow. The mental faculties are unaffected until the disease is advanced. The general picture of someone with Parkinson's disease shows the back bent, the chin poking forward, the arms held rigidly by the sides, and the hands stiff and trembling. Bent hips and knees tend to throw the weight forward, making the person unsteady.

Treatment is directed toward relieving discomfort and prolonging activity. Water activities may be a good form of physiotherapy that helps increase movement and maintain independence by delaying further stiffening and movement limitation. Warm water activities also help relax rigid muscles. Walking in the water, stopping and starting exercises, and getting into and out of the pool may help promote greater agility. It is very important not to hurry those who have Parkinson's disease.

During any type of movement, balance is a problem for these students. Adequate support should be available at all times, which may mean providing assistance during pool entry and exit and in the locker room.

Perthes Disease

Perthes disease is caused by demineralization of the bone and is characterized by deformity or abnormal growth of the hipbone. Depending on the amount of involvement, one or both lower extremities may be unable to bear weight.

Aquatics instructors should check with the student's physical therapist so that counterindicated activity is avoided. An approved, individual educational, rehabilitative, or medical plan should be set up for each student.

Poliomyelitis

Poliomyelitis, also known as infantile paralysis, is a viral infection that can destroy the cells of the spinal cord and cause spotty weakness of muscles. It can result in muscle weakness or partial paralysis.

Polio has almost been eliminated in the United States, but vaccinations are still given regularly because some new cases occur each year. However, it caused so many orthopedic disabilities in the past that aquatics instructors still occasionally encounter a disabled student who had polio many years ago.

Rubella Syndrome

When a woman contracts rubella (German measles) during the first 3 months of pregnancy, the viral organism is likely to be passed to her unborn child, causing mental retardation, blindness, deafness, or multiple impairments. Cataracts, heart disease, and microcephaly also have been associated with first-trimester rubella.

Assistive, tactile, kinesthetic, and sensory awareness methods are effective in teaching those who have rubella syndrome. Recommendations from the health care team or physician are helpful in formulating individualized teaching plans.

Sensory Impairments

People can have one or a combination of sensory disabilities. Sensory disabilities include hearing impairments, deafness, visual impairments, blindness, and combined deafness and blindness.

People with hearing impairments are found in every community, although few are totally deaf. Deafness can be congenital or acquired. Congenital deafness can occur before birth or in the first months after birth. A congenitally deaf person either has never heard sound or language or does not remember it at all. Speech is taught through imitation, usually starting at a young age, so that the individual can develop physically, intellectually, and emotionally to the fullest extent possible.

Water skills can be taught to the hearing impaired person either orally, when possible, or manually. Often a combination of these approaches works well. When the student has been taught how to listen and pay attention, speaking slowly and making certain the student understands what is being said may be sufficient. Hard-of-hearing students may lose contact with the instructor if their attention is distracted. Affection and patience are essential teaching components. Knowledge of sign language is helpful, and in some cases, an interpreter may be needed.

When the hearing loss itself is not correctable, the aim of school and recreational activities should be to minimize educational and psychosocial consequences of the hearing impairment. Surgery or medication are ineffective in treating sensorineural or central hearing losses. However, conductive types of hearing loss can be at least partially corrected through surgery or medication. Instructors should know how severe the hearing loss is in an individual student and whether that student can read lips, can sign, or wears a hearing aid. This can help in formulating appropriate communication techniques in the swimming pool.

More than half of the people who are called blind have partial vision. Only about 2 in every 1,000 people are legally blind, and more than half of them are over 65. Water activities help the blind learn to move about freely in a relatively strange environment, and the water is a great medium for socializing.

Instructing the blind requires the use of words and sensations. Many visually impaired and most hearing impaired students can be mainstreamed readily. Loss of vision in one eye may be accompanied by loss of the ability to see in three dimensions and loss of equilibrium. Water exercises and activities may be prescribed by team members to help individuals overcome these impairments.

Visually impaired students should be completely oriented to all facilities, such as the bathrooms and the pool, both shallow and deep ends. Before they enter the water they should learn where various objects are and where certain sounds come from. They should have as much independence as possible but should be very carefully supervised. A student can use an instructor's or assistant's arm for guidance when walking.

In the first stages of instruction, the student's head should be out of the water as much as possible, since water minimizes sound and the blind student relies heavily on sound. The instructor or an assistant should be within body contact in the learning stages to help the student feel secure. Arms and legs can be guided when demonstrating a skill.

A sounding device located at the shallow end of the pool provides constant orientation. Vision plays a central role in establishing locomotion and mobility skills. Activities such as swimming help the student establish or improve such skills in other ways. Water activities encourage the young student or the newly visually impaired person to explore and investigate the environment. Blindisms, such as rhythmic swaying, arms waving, and twisting and turning of the body, may substitute for outwardly oriented exploration of the environment. Optical aids are an important medical intervention for the partially sighted person.

Some participants may be deaf and blind. Aquatics activities offer such students a flexible medium for learning, aiding in emotional and social growth and development. Aquatics also enhance socialization, communication, and motor skills.

Blind-deaf students may react with fear, withdrawal, hyperexcitability, and emotional stress to a new situation. They must be made aware through touch that they are not isolated. Body awareness and the awareness of spatial relationships are a first step in learning about the water and what movements can be performed in the water. To start, fundamental movements can be learned and explored; then sequences of motor activities—the use of simple objects and equipment—can be learned.

Instructors can help the participant learn by performing identical movements with the student, presenting objects to the student, helping the student imitate the desired movement, and guiding the student in using the objects and movements. The participant may be apathetic, overly cautious, or completely resistant. Patience is essential. The student will thrive on sensory stimulation, exciting (not frightening) movement, and security. Developing directionality is essential because the student can neither see nor hear what is going on. Orientation and water adjustment should be thoroughly learned and practiced.

Communication with a person who is both blind and deaf is not difficult. When approaching these students, the instructor should let them know he or she is near with a warm, friendly touch such as a firm handshake. Gestures should be gentle and positive, not abrupt. The instructor should work out a signal to identify himself or herself and learn from the students' parents, teachers, and friends how best to communicate. Students should be encouraged to use their voice, if they have speech, and should be told when they can speak if there are others present. Students should also be kept informed of their whereabouts and told when the instructor is leaving, being left in a safe and comfortable situation. The instructor should keep sufficiently close to let students know he or she is there and should let students take an arm when walking. Simple signals can tell students to go upstairs, go downstairs, walk through a doorway, or board a vehicle. Students should be encouraged to use their own ability and express their own ideas.

Spina Bifida

Spina bifida is a birth defect that occurs in close to 2 out of every 1,000 live births. Its cause is unknown. One or more of the individual bones of the back (vertebrae) fail to close completely, leaving a cleft or defect. Contents of the spinal canal can slip through this opening, similar to what happens with a hernia. This produces a sac, called a *myelomeningocele* , that is covered with a fragile membrane that can be damaged easily. If nerves are damaged, paralysis and infection can result.

Without treatment, 60 percent of those born with spina bifida will die, primarily because of infection that spreads through the cerebrospinal fluid. But even babies born severely disabled have a chance to survive because of medical progress and modern surgery, usually performed within 24 hours after birth.

Physical conditions imposed by spina bifida vary widely. The majority of people with spina bifida rely on braces, crutches, and wheelchairs. Some lack bladder and bowel control and may require a catheter. Others may have a hydrocephalic condition (water on the brain) or visual defects. Many participate in water activity programs.

Precautions should be taken to prevent contamination of the swimming area that may lead to infection. The pool water should be checked often to see that it meets sanitary standards, and students should clamp off catheters and secure colostomies before entering the pool.

Spinal and Postural Deviations

Among the most common causes of spinal and postural deviations are the following:

- The aftermath of polio, which may have left some muscles too weak to balance the pull of the remaining, stronger muscles.
- Bad postural habits or patterns, both in motion and while standing still.
- Other conditions of unknown origin that have left muscles on one side of the spine stronger than muscles on the directly opposite side.

Spinal deviation, seen both in children and adults, may be classified as functional or structural. In functional deviations, the bones are still moveable and the curve often can be straightened. In structural deviation, the curve is permanent. A curve may progress quickly or slowly; it may be severe, mild, or in between.

Aquatics activities, besides providing general recreation, may cause bilateral strengthening, decrease the curve, or prevent or retard further curve progression. Strokes in which the limbs on both sides are working together—symmetrical strokes such as the breaststroke or a modified backstroke—work well.

Spinal Cord Injuries

When a person receives a spinal cord injury, the communications network between the brain and certain parts of the body is cut and messages no longer flow past the damaged area. The seriousness of the communications breakdown depends on the severity and location of the injury.

The human spinal cord is a bundle of nerve cells and fibers approximately 17 inches long that extends from the brain to the body's muscles, internal organs, and skin. It relays messages from the brain to all parts of the body and back again. The spinal cord is protected by 33 vertebrae: 7 vertebrae in the neck, 12 thoracic vertebrae in the chest, 5 lumbar vertebrae in the back, 5 sacral vertebrae in the lower back, and 4 vertebrae in the tailbone.

There are different levels of spinal cord injury. Generally, the higher the level of injury, the greater the disability. For example, an injury to the spine in the cervical area (neck) can cause paralysis in both arms and legs and result in quadriplegia, while a lower injury, such as at the thoracic or chest level, can affect the legs and lower parts of the body and result in paraplegia. An injury to the spinal cord is labeled by the specific area involved.

The section of the spinal cord that is damaged determines what type of movement and sensation will be retained by the injured person. Injuries are classified as "complete" or "incomplete," although the results of every injury are unique. In a complete injury there is total loss of muscle power and sensation below the level of injury, while an incomplete injury does not cause total loss of motor power and sensation. Whatever the level of injury is, it is important to effectively maximize the degree of functioning that remains.

A spinal cord injury may result in either no sensation or less sensation in certain body parts. In addition to loss of movement and feeling, other bodily functions may be affected. With proper medical and self-care, however, a number of complications can be prevented. Knowledge of the disability and of how to deal with physical problems as they arise will help enable the individual to live a full and active life.

Rehabilitation is a word used frequently in the months following an injury. It is a specialty concerned with returning an individual to an active and productive life. The primary objective of a rehabilitation program is to enable the individual to reach a maximum level of independent functioning. The newly injured learn activities of daily life and self-care.

Swimming is one of the activities often introduced into the rehabilitative program. Because each student should have an individual program plan, it is recommended that those working with spinal cord injuries cooperate with a rehabilitation center or hospital in developing the program. Some hospitals have pools, and other community resources may be available.

Institutes and Training

Aquatics for special populations has three levels of YMCA training: aquatic director/administrator, aquatic specialist instructor/leader for special populations, and aquatic assistant. Any of these positions may be filled by either paid professionals or certified volunteers.

An aquatic director/administrator must be at least 20 years old and must have a minimum of 2 hours of orientation through the specialist course in aquatics for special populations. In addition, the candidate must have at least 10 hours of practical experience working with people who have disabilities and must have completed the YMCA Basic Aquatic Leadership Course. Certification is available to those holding YMCA prerequisite training as aquatic directors, aquatic instructors, or swimming instructors, or to volunteer leaders who have the necessary training. People with certifications from other organizations should check with their aquatic director or other authorized personnel to see if there is a reciprocal agreement with the YMCA.

A YMCA aquatic specialist instructor/leader for special populations (formerly called swimming for the handicapped) must be at least 17 years old and must have at least 10 hours of practical preservice experience plus the specialist course. An aquatic assistant must be at least 15 years old and must receive the same special training as the specialist instructor/leader. Certification in lifesaving is not a requirement.

This chapter consists of outlines of the training for aquatic directors/administrators and aquatic specialist instructors/leaders plus the Guidance Checklist for Facility Accessibility that is used as part of these training courses.

YMCA Aquatic Directors and Administrators Orientation

The orientation is a 2-hour course that prepares candidates for the position of aquatic director/administrator for aquatics for special populations programs.

I. Administration of program
   A. Need
      1. Surveying health agencies, school districts, child-find programs, service agencies, associations, and special interest groups
      2. Analyzing need for community-based programs for special populations, number of potential clients, facilities, and personnel
      3. Organizing data
         a) Number of participants according to ability and age
         b) Types of individuals to be served
         c) Various kinds of classes to be organized for instruction, recreation, therapy, leisure education, and competition (Programs should be developed one at a time, then expanded.)
         d) Class locations such as schools, hospitals, public and private institutions, and agencies
      4. Knowing requirements for training personnel

   B. Staff and training
      1. Adequate number of professional staff and volunteers to supervise and instruct preservice, in-service, and direct service programs

2. Provision for both formal and informal training of all support personnel
3. Standards
    a) At least one staff person per program certified in aquatics for special populations or its equivalent
    b) A sufficient number of aquatic leaders
    c) Additional trained volunteers as needed
    d) A supervisor trained in CPR, first aid, and lifesaving

C. Scheduling
    1. Time
        a) Adequate program time to include locker room, dressing and undressing (about 15 minutes each), and shower use (about 5 minutes) preceeding and following water session
        b) Length of class and time of day to depend on schedules of individual participants and availability of transportation
    2. Space—accessibility (See Guidance Checklist, p. 113.)
        a) Parking
        b) Ramps
        c) Building entrance
        d) Rest rooms
        e) Dressing area
        f) Showers
        g) Swimming area
    3. Facility
        a) Suitable aquatics area, maintained at conditions best for program participants
        b) Specialized equipment for lifting and transferring participants in dressing, shower, and water areas
        c) Emergency signals in all areas

D. Public relations and marketing (See Public Relations section, p. 8.)
    1. Reaching the public through organizations, schools, churches, and print and electronic media
    2. Distributing information through pamphlets, schedules, brochures, press releases, and speaking engagements, using YMCA brochures and media resources from other programs

E. Financing
1. Staff costs to depend on personnel needed, paid and volunteer
2. Pool costs to depend on individual pool expenses
3. Equipment costs to be kept at a minimum by using innovative material
4. Marketing and promotional costs to be kept at a minimum by using public service news media (All promotional material should be of professional quality.)
5. Funding suggestions
   a) Program service fees
   b) Memberships
   c) Scholarships
   d) Individual donations
   e) Bequests and memorials
   f) Group donations
   g) City, county, and state funds
   h) School funds
   i) Exchanges of facility privileges with other organizations
   j) Private foundations
   k) Federal funding
   l) Federated funding
   m) Other
F. Evaluating the program
1. Collecting data—supplying feedback to advisory groups, board of directors, aquatics committee, professional members of team, and other staff members
   a) Social and water skill development
   b) Frequent staff evaluation
   c) Quarterly program evaluation done by staff, participants, family, and consultants
   d) Evaluation of impact on community through marketing and communications channels
2. Information
   a) Background information on participants—doctors and allied medical personnel, schools, families, social and health agencies, and any other necessary parties
   b) Daily reports from instructional staff on attendance; records of age, sex, and type of condition;

individual progress reports (Reports should be computerized if possible.)

3. Statistics and reports
   a) Computer services and networking between main Y and branches
   b) Graphs and skill sheets
   c) Types of conditions of participants
   d) Ages, sexes, and ethnic backgrounds
   e) Social awareness changes
   f) Skill improvement
   g) Number of paid staff and volunteer staff
   h) Program impact on community
   i) Inter- and intra-agency communication and networking
   j) Communication among professionals
   k) Carry over of values into school, home, and community
4. Evaluation and publicity material
   a) Letters to support team, funding agencies, boards, community, and other groups
   b) Reports to support team, funding agencies, and other groups
   c) Brochures to funding agencies, community, media, and other groups
   d) Press releases and public service announcements
   e) Speakers for community groups

II. Practical experience
   A. Work with various types of disabilities and conditions (Simulation techniques may be used.)
   B. View slides, films, and videotapes about various conditions and program content
   C. Prepare Individual Educational Plans and program plans and evaluations

III. Interpretive materials
   A. Outlines
      1. Program organization and administration
      2. Descriptions and definitions
      3. Teaching suggestions
   B. Forms
      1. Institute application
      2. Program participation application
      3. Physicians' forms

4. Parents' forms
5. Other forms
6. Skill sheets
7. Evaluation forms—program and participant

C. Materials for distribution
   1. Guidelines for director/administrator
   2. Director/administrator seminar outline
   3. Guidelines for aquatics institutes

D. Institute supplies
   1. Text—*Aquatics for Special Populations; MAY* (Mainstreaming Activities for Youth, Volumes I, II, III, and IV) (Contact the YMCA Office of Special Populations or the Y Program Store.)
   2. Equipment for simulation activities
      a) Triangular bandages to use as blindfolds and to restrict movement
      b) Wheelchairs, crutches, earplugs, prosthetic devices, hearing aids, and blackened glasses
      c) Records, equipment, or other resources from local groups for the disabled, health suppliers, hospitals, and rehabilitation programs
   3. Films and audiovisuals (See also Appendix A, Bibliography.)
      a) "Splash," Documentary Films, 3217 Trout Gulch Road, Aptos, CA 95003
      b) "Swimming for a Congenital Quad Amputee," Instructional Media Center, University of Texas, University Station, Austin, TX 78712
      c) "Swimming for the Handicapped," Muscular Dystrophy Association of America, 1790 Broadway, New York, NY
      d) "Focus on Ability," contact local American Red Cross chapter for information
      e) Resource material from National Epilepsy Foundation, Alzheimer's Foundation, and other organizations

YMCA Aquatic Specialist Instructor/Leader for Special Populations Institute

This 24- to 26-hour course includes preservice orientation, class work, and water work. It prepares candidates for the position of aquatic specialist instructor/leader for special populations. An advanced aquatic specialist instructor seminar for special populations currently is being developed. For more information contact the Office of Special Populations at PO Box 1781, Longview, WA 98632 or (206) 577-0243.

Institute Time Guidelines

Minimum time	Content
1 hour	I. Introduction A. Welcome B. Introduction C. Review of course materials
1½ hours	II. Curriculum content A. Overview of program
1½ hours	B. Program organization and administration
	C. Types of disabilities
	D. Community referrals
10 hours	E. Teaching methods and practical experience (lectures, discussion, audiovisuals, and practice)
2 hours	III. Small group discussions (videotape if possible)
6-8 hours	IV. Water work, preferably with participants (videotape if possible)

2 hours or more

24-26 hours for institute

V. Theoretical examination on site or to take home (water practicum on site during institute)

Specialist Instructor/Leader Institute

I. Introduction
    A. Welcome
        1. By executive director
        2. By community leader
        3. By institute director
        4. By board member
        5. By program participant
    B. Introduction (individual expectations for institute)
    C. Review of course materials (handouts, local information, training schedule, and videotapes)
II. Curriculum content
    A. Overview of program
        1. Why program is needed (audiovisual, overhead projector, transparencies)
            a) Available statistics on impairments, disabilities, and handicaps
            b) Individualized programs, segregated versus integrated classes
        2. Who needs program
            a) Aquatics beneficial to disabled and nondisabled
            b) Start with segregated programs, build toward mainstreaming; some begin with integrated programs
        3. Psychological benefits of specialized program
            a) Opportunity for success and building confidence
            b) Development of social awareness
            c) Opportunity to grow through new experiences
            d) Improvements of self-image and physical skills
        4. Physical benefits of specialized program
            a) Most people can participate
            b) Opportunities for movement that are not available on land
        5. Purposes of aquatics programs
            a) Educational
            b) Recreational

      c) Social
      d) Rehabilitative
      e) Habilitative
      f) Competitive
      g) Fun

B. Program organization and administration
    1. Advisory committee
        a) As complete a cross section of the community as possible
           (1) People interested in service
           (2) People knowledgeable about various disabilities
               (a) Physicians, psychologists, therapists, and allied health professionals
               (b) Social workers
               (c) Teachers
               (d) Parents
               (e) Participants (consumers)
           (3) Members from community at large
               (a) Community agencies
               (b) Service clubs
               (c) Church groups
               (d) Lodges
               (e) Youth groups
               (f) Groups representing various disabilities
               (g) Court referrals
               (h) Voluntary action centers
               (i) Retired senior volunteer program (RSVP)
           (4) Other interested personnel/potential team members
               (a) Program participants
               (b) Youth agencies that work with the disabled
               (c) Physical education teachers
               (d) Special education teachers
               (e) School board members
               (f) Recreation staffs
               (g) College and university personnel
               (h) Parents/guardians
               (i) Medical/allied medical personnel
               (j) Community recreation directors/staff
               (k) Other YMCA professionals

2. Determining community need
    a) Estimating number of participants by survey through health agencies, schools, county and state health departments, agencies related to specific disabilities, and service providers
        (1) Ability level (age appropriate)
        (2) Mental and chronological age
    b) News articles and other media information
    c) Kinds of classes
        (1) For instruction, recreation, and leisure time
        (2) In schools, hospitals, or institutions
        (3) For therapy under direction of therapist
        (4) For families and extended families
        (5) For other organized groups
        (6) When need is ascertained, one program success developed at a time, then expanded
3. Aquatic instructors
    a) Adequate number of aquatic instructors/volunteers, trained or willing to be trained
    b) Ratios to depend on individuals and programs
    c) Skills required in addition to that of swimming instruction
        (1) Knowledge of special conditions and ability to network, ask questions, and obtain answers from knowledgeable people
        (2) Initiative and imagination
        (3) Patience and understanding
        (4) Ability to develop Individualized Program Plans and Individualized Educational Plans
        (5) Teaching ability
    d) Value of volunteer program
        (1) Develops person-to-person and teaching skills of volunteers
        (2) Develops community resources
        (3) Develops community interest
        (4) Helps maintain adequate budget
        (5) Builds community interest in YMCA
    e) Sources of personnel
        (1) Trained and certified aquatics leadership
        (2) High school and college students
        (3) Members of community
        (4) Parents/families/friends

   (5) Retired individuals

   (6) Consumers, participants, and others

4. Training of associated personnel

  a) Transportation—lifts and transfers

  b) Locker room and shower area

  c) Records

  d) Aquatic assistants

  e) Evaluators

5. Training of volunteer help

  a) Several sessions of lecture and water work

  b) Discussion of the importance of volunteers

  c) Education in awareness of disabilities

   (1) Background material on aquatics orientation

   (2) Description of swim skills to be used and adaptations

   (3) Lectures by persons with disabilities who are good speakers

  d) Encouragement of volunteers to take YMCA certification courses

  e) Follow-up of the in-service training

   (1) Meeting with instructors, volunteers, and other members of advisory committee

   (2) Reviewing swimming progressions and adaptations

   (3) Looking for new material

   (4) Planning field trips

   (5) Attending seminars, institutes, and other programs, both inter- and intra-agency

  f) Materials for training

   (1) Films, manuals, and associated material on disabilities and swimming

   (2) Audiovisual aids

   (3) Meetings with special interest groups for additional information

6. Cooperation of medical and allied professionals

7. Safety

  a) First aid, CPR, and treatment of seizures

  b) Emergency procedures and operation of safety equipment

  c) Maintenance and use of aquatics records

  d) Common effects of medication

  e) Requirements of special conditions

8. Water conditions
   a) Water temperature 83 degrees and above, air temperature 2 to 5 degrees higher
   b) Suggested water depth—3 to 5 feet
   c) Chemical balance at proper, healthful levels
9. Recommended facilities and equipment
   a) Accessibility (See Guidance Checklist, p. 113.)
      (1) Adequate, accessible parking, properly marked with universal handicapped symbol
      (2) Dressing and locker rooms adjacent to swim area, accessible from street level by wheelchair
      (3) Minimum of two dressing rooms and locker rooms
      (4) Rest rooms equipped for wheelchairs and in close proximity to the water activity area
      (5) Area adapted to wheelchair level
   b) Equipment
      (1) ramps, transfer tiers, steps, hoists, plinths, and chair lifts
      (2) Adapted shower facilities
      (3) Games, toys, and novel items
      (4) Parallel bars, benches, or seats in the water
      (5) Mats for deck exercise and emergency situations (seizures)
10. Records and evaluations
    a) Written data on students compiled before class starts from medical personnel, parents/guardians, educators, service providers, and participants, providing detailed profile for setting skills, progressions, and goals for each student
    b) Records completed and kept confidential and available only to team members
    c) Accurate daily records and evaluations maintained (Attendance records and accident forms should be kept for 7 years. Records and information on individual progress of participants also should be kept.)
    d) Professional advisors asked direct questions about each student's abilities and potential
    e) Application forms, certification forms, progress sheets, and other forms developed for each program (See p. 125.)

    f) Program and attendance statistics kept accurately

    g) Evaluations made measuring fitness, skills, and development

     (1) Physical fitness and ability to perform skills

     (2) Social aspects—ability to work individually, to work in a group, and to relate to people of various ages and skills

    h) Information shared when appropriate with consultants, referring agencies, teachers, families, and participants

  11. Aquatics procedures

    a) Established procedure for each class enhancing program stability

    b) Program procedures for beginners

     (1) Checking student records before class

     (2) Planning adequate time for dressing and showering

     (3) Leading students to shallow end of pool

     (4) Entering pool correctly

     (5) Instructing group

     (6) Working on individual program and swim skills

     (7) Playing group games

     (8) Giving class some free time

     (9) Dismissing class

     (10) Completing records

     (11) Evaluating progress with staff

    c) Water area divided according to student abilities (Water area may be used by more than one class at a time, promoting mainstreaming.)

 C. Types of disabilities

  1. Mental impairments, disabilities, and handicaps

  2. Physical impairments, disabilities, and handicaps

  3. Multiple disabilities

  4. Emotional disabilities

  5. Learning problems—may be caused by motor disability, perceptual disability, incomprehension, lack of motivation, or inability to work with individual instructor

 D. Community referrals

  1. Group homes

  2. Foster homes

  3. Independent living centers

4. Substance abuse programs
5. Court referrals
6. Programs on aging
E. Teaching methods and practical experience
  1. Objectives
    a) To teach principles of water safety and aquatics skill development
    b) To assist in rehabilitation or habilitation of individuals
      (1) opportunity for social approval
      (2) opportunity for adjustment to condition
      (3) help in overcoming self-consciousness
      (4) development of physical fitness
      (5) a chance to succeed and increase self-esteem—valuable for normalization and mainstreaming
  2. Value of water activities
    a) Improved physical and mental health
    b) Education through recreation in which many can participate
    c) Skill development for leisure time pursuits
    d) Opportunity for socializing and fun
  3. Communication
    a) Vocabulary
    b) Body movements
    c) Verbal and nonverbal communication
  4. Teaching hints
    a) Orienting students to building and aquatic facility, establishing trust
    b) Motivating students
    c) Using consistency in discipline
    d) Emphasizing safety and emergency procedures
    e) Teaching adaptations and innovations
      (1) Providing individual assistance when necessary
      (2) Promoting independence
      (3) Reinforcing correct behavior immediately
      (4) Repeating skills to be mastered using various approaches
      (5) Helping make skills an automatic response
      (6) Being flexible, making adjustments as needed

(7) Being creative, using new teaching techniques
    (a) Movement exploration
    (b) Games
    (c) Station-to-station training
    (d) Circuit training
    (e) Interval training
    f) Practicing planning and conducting a class
    g) Evaluating
III. Small group discussion (idea and information exchange sessions and evaluation)
IV. Water work
V. Theoretical examination on site or to take home

Guidance Checklist for Facility Accessibility

Facility accessibility is essential for developing and providing facilities and programs for individuals with special needs. A properly designed facility promotes use by such individuals. Studies indicate that approximately 50 million Americans have physical, mental, and/or communication disabilities.

Federal standards require facilities that receive federal funding to provide program areas accessible to individuals with disabilities. The Building and Furnishings Service of the YMCA of the USA, now known as BFS, has as its goal to ensure that all new or renovated facilities be accessible to everyone.

The Office of Special Populations and BFS have prepared the following accessibility checklist, providing initial guidance to making a facility compatible with the needs of participants with disabilities.

Universal Handicapped Symbol

_____ Approaching a facility can be a concern to those who have disabilities. Some facilities are small and the entrance is obvious. In a large complex building or facility, however, the entrances and exits need to be properly marked with the universal handicapped symbol.

Parking Area

_____ The universal symbol identifying an accessible parking area and directional arrows pointing the way should be visible.

_____ The incline of any ramp should be 1 inch rise in 12 inches of run and in close proximity to the accessible facility entrance.

_____ Ramping from the parking area to the building entry should not contain curbing.

Passenger Arrival or Departure Space

_____ Unloading and loading areas should be in an unobstructed area and clearly indicated.

Door and Passageways

_____ Entry areas with revolving doors should have an alternate access for wheelchairs.

_____ Doors with easy-to-grasp handles a minimum of 32 inches wide and thresholds no higher than ½ inch high should be provided

_____ Passageways of 48 inches clear width should be available.

_____ Signs stating that the building meets handicap accessibility requirements should be visible.

_____ Special hardware on the entry door or automatic controls for doors should be accessible to the disabled individual.

_____ Grab bars or handrails should be available for individuals with balance problems.

_____ Floor surfaces should be smooth and hard surfaced or covered with a tightly woven slip-resistant carpet.

Stairs

_____ Stairs should have a nonslip surface with handrails on both sides.

_____ Steps should have 12-inch treads and 6-inch risers.

Ramps

_____ Ramps should have no sloping greater than 1 inch in 12 inches.

_____ Handrails on both sides should be 32 inches from the surface and extend 1 foot beyond the top and bottom of the ramp.

_____ Platforms should be built at least every 30 feet for long ramps or walks with a threshold of no more than ½ inch.

Telephones

_____ At least one telephone should be provided and mounted so there are 54 inches to the top side reach and 48 inches to the top forward reach.

Communication Signals

_____ Communication signals for the hearing and visually impaired should be both audible and visible, providing a safe environment.

_____ Raised and braille numbers and letters should identify rooms and exits.

Elevators

_____ Buildings with more than one floor should have an elevator with directional signs visible from the entrance.

_____ Controls should be set low and identified in braille.

Drinking Fountains

_____ At least one fountain should be provided, mounted so that the spout height is a maximum of 36 inches.

Meeting and Activity Rooms

_____ Room identification should be provided for the blind.

_____ Doorways should have a minimum of 32-inches clearance to accommodate a wheelchair.

Rest Rooms

_____ Rest rooms should be clearly marked with the universal handicapped symbol at the entrance to show accessibility.

_____ The entrance must be a minimum of 32 inches wide and the stall 5 feet deep.

_____ The door should swing out.

_____ The toilet seat should be set 17 to 19 inches from the floor with grab bars on both sides.

_____ Easy-to-operate (lever-type) faucets should be provided.

_____ One sink/lavatory should be hung 29 inches from the floor.

_____ Accessories (towel dispensers and mirrors) should be hung 40 inches from the floor to the bottom edge.

Showers and Locker Rooms

_____ Showers and locker rooms should be located on entry level and adjacent to the pool; openings should be of sufficient width for clearance with handrails on both sides.

_____ A stationary seat for mobility impaired participants should be provided.

_____ Faucets should be mounted 48 inches from the floor.

_____ Wheelchair-height lockers and hooks should be provided.

_____ The locker room should include seating space and a dressing table area large enough to facilitate an adult's changing clothes.

Pool Areas

_____ Pool areas should have steps with 12-inch treads, 6-inch risers, and 2 railings.

_____ Built-in ramps/steps are ideal but costly; portable ramps/steps are an alternative.

_____ A permanent or moveable lift or hoist should be available for people requiring assistance.

_____ Depth markings should be indicated on both sides of the pool.

_____ The water level should be flush with the deck.

_____ Provisions for higher water temperatures should be available.

_____ The pool should be located adjacent to a barrier-free shower and locker room.

Emergency Signals

_____ Consideration should be given to providing separate visible and audible emergency signals such as buttons and alarms.

This accessibility checklist is a guideline representing minimum standards. For information about renovating or planning a new facility, contact the BFS of the YMCA of the USA at 101 N. Wacker Drive, Chicago, IL 60606 or call (312) 269-0525.

Appendix **A**
Bibliography

Adapted Physical Education

Arnheim, D.D., & Sinclair, W.A. (1985). *Physical education for special populations: A developmental, adapted and remedial approach.* Englewood Cliffs, NJ: Prentice-Hall.

Auxter, D., & Pyfer, J. (1985). *Principles and methods of adapted physical education and recreation.* St. Louis, MO: Times Mirror/Mosby College Publishing.

Bigge, J.L. (1982). *Teaching individuals with physical and multiple disabilities.* Columbus, OH: Charles E. Merrill.

Bundschuh, E. (1983). *Project Dart: Physical education for handicapped students.* Northbrook, IL: Hubbard.

Davis, E. (1968, May). Fresh approaches for combating persistent problems. *Challenge.* Washington, DC: American Alliance for Health, Physical Education, Recreation and Dance.

Geddes, D. (1978). *Physical activities for individuals with handicapping conditions.* St. Louis, MO: C.V. Mosby.

Hill, K. (1976). *Dance for physically disabled persons.* Reston, VA: Information and Research Utilization Center. (Available from IRUC, 1900 Association Drive, Reston, VA 22091.)

Reynolds, G.D., & Dedrick, E.O. (1973). *Adaptive programming by the YMCA for people with special needs.* Longview, WA: Office of Special Populations, YMCA of the USA. (Available from Office of Special Populations, YMCA of the USA, P.O. Box 1781, Longview, WA 98632.)

Sherrill, C. (1981). *Adapted physical education and recreation: A multidisciplinary approach.* Dubuque, IA: William C. Brown Company.

Vinland National Center (1985). *An introduction to fitness with persons who are disabled.* Loretto, MN: Author.

Aquatics

American National Red Cross. (1974). *Swimming for the handicapped: A manual for the aide.* Washington, DC: Author.

American National Red Cross. (1977). *Adapted aquatics* (1st ed.). Garden City, NY: Doubleday.

Campion, M.R. (1985). *Hydrotherapy in pediatrics.* Rockville, MD: Aspen Systems Corporation.

Council for National Cooperation in Aquatics. (1967-1974). *Proceedings of the Council for National Cooperation in Aquatics.* Indianapolis, IN: Author. (Available from Council for National Cooperation in Aquatics, 9701 Harbor Court, Indianapolis, IN 46229.)

Council for National Cooperation in Aquatics. (1969). *A practical guide for teaching the mentally retarded to swim.* Washington, DC: American Alliance for Health, Physical Education and Recreation.

Heckathorn, J. (1980). *Strokes and strokes.* Reston, VA: American Alliance for Health, Physical Education, Recreation and Dance. (Available from AAHPERD, 1900 Association Drive, Reston, VA 22091.)

Katz, J. (1985). *The W.E.T. workout.* New York: Facts on File Publications.

Krasevec, J.A., & Grimes, D.C. (1984). *Hydrorobics.* New York: Leisure Press. (Available from Human Kinetics Publishers, Box 5076, Champaign, IL 61820.)

Lee, T. (1984). *Aquacises: Terry Lee's water workout book.* Reston, VA: Prentice-Hall.

Melvin, L. (1976). *Aquatic games and swimming techniques for the handicapped.* Atlanta, GA: Georgia Department of Human Resources, Division of Mental Health and Mental Retardation.

National Association for Girls and Women in Sport. (1980). *Sports medicine meets synchronized swimming.* Reston, VA: The American Alliance for Health, Physical Education, Recreation and Dance. (Available from AAHPERD, 1900 Association Drive, Reston, VA 22091.)

President's Council on Physical Fitness and Sports. (1977). *Aquatic dynamics: Physical fitness and sports.* Washington, DC: U.S. Government Printing Office.

Reynolds, G.D. (1973). *A swimming program for the handicapped.* New York: Association Press.

Reynolds, G.D. (1976). *Agency development of aquatic programs for special populations.* Alexandria, VA: National Recreation and Park Association.

Reynolds, G.D. (1979). Mainstreaming your aquatics program. *Aquatics Guide: Tips and Techniques for Teachers and Coaches.* Washington, DC: National Association for Girls and Women in Sport.

Reynolds, G.D. (1970). Swimming: A vehicle for rehabilitation of the mentally retarded. In L.L. Neal (Ed.), *Recreation's role in the rehabilitation of the mentally retarded.* Eugene, OR: University of Oregon, Department of Special Education. (Available from Office of Special Populations, YMCA of the USA, P.O. Box 1781, Longview, WA 98632.)

YMCA of the USA. (1982). *Physical fitness through water exercise.* Chicago: Author.

YMCA of the USA and the Arthritis Foundation. (1985). *Arthritis Foundation YMCA aquatic program.* Champaign, IL: Human Kinetics.

Equipment and Facilities

Nesbitt, J.A. (Ed.). (1986). *The international directory of recreation—oriented assistive device sources.* Marina Del Rey, CA: Lifeboat Press.

Porter, J. (1979). *Equipment and facilities.* Parkersburg, WV: Regional Education Service Agency.

Specifications for making buildings and facilities accessible to and usable by physically handicapped people. (1980). New York: ANSI. (ANSI-A117.1) (Available from ANSI, 1430 Broadway, New York, NY 10018.)

YMCA of the USA. (1986). *Planning for a barrier-free environment.* Longview, WA: Office of Special Populations, YMCA of the USA. (Available from Office of Special Populations, YMCA of the USA, P.O. Box 1781, Longview, WA 98632.)

Mainstreaming

Reynolds, G.D. (Ed.). (1978). *Outline for a successful program for mainstreaming special populations through aquatic programs.* Longview, WA: Office of Special Populations, YMCA of the USA. (Available from Office of Special Populations, YMCA of the USA, P.O. Box 1781, Longview, WA 98632.)

Reynolds, G.D. (Ed.). (1981). *Mainstreaming, book 1, personal values.* Longview, WA: Office of Special Populations, YMCA of the USA. (Available in microfilm from ERIC Clearinghouse on Handicapped and Gifted Children, 1920 Association Drive, Reston, VA 22091.)

Reynolds, G.D. (Ed.). (1981). *Mainstreaming, book 2, guide to developing a program.* Longview, WA: Office of Special Populations, YMCA of the USA. (Available in microfilm from ERIC Clearinghouse on Handicapped and Gifted Children, 1920 Association Drive, Reston, VA 22091.)

Reynolds, G.D. (Ed.), (1981). *Mainstreaming, book 3, your personal guide.* Longview, WA: Office of Special Populations, YMCA of the USA. (Available in microfilm from ERIC Clearinghouse on Handicapped and Gifted Children, 1920 Association Drive, Reston, VA 22091.)

Reynolds, G.D., & Jenkins, D. (Eds.). (1983). *A workshop guide: Mainstreaming awareness in youth serving agencies.* Longview, WA: Northwest Education Materials Association.

Physical Activity

Bailey, C. (1978). *Fit or fat: A new way to health and fitness through nutrition and aerobic exercise.* Boston: Houghton Mifflin.

DiGennaro, J. (1983). *The new physical fitness: Exercise for everybody.* Englewood, CO: Morton Publishing.

Godfrey, B.B., & Kephart, N.E. (1969). *Movement patterns and motor education.* New York: Appleton-Century-Crofts.

Rarick, G.L. (1973). *Physical activity, human growth and development.* New York: Academic Press.

Stillwell, J.L., & Stockard, J.R. (1983). *Fitness exercises for children.* New York: Leisure Press. (Available from Human Kinetics Publishers, Box 5076, Champaign, IL 61820.)

Special Populations

Auster, D. *Special olympics research projects.* Washington, DC: Joseph P. Kennedy, Jr., Foundation.

Dennis, W. (1979). *What every physical educator should know about asthma.* Denver, CO: American Lung Association.

Hayden, F.J. (1964). *Physical fitness for the mentally retarded.* Ontario, Canada: Metropolitan Toronto Association for Retarded Children.

Hirst, C., & Michaelis, E. (1984). *Retarded kids need to play.* New York: Leisure Press. (Available from Human Kinetics Publishers, Box 5076, Champaign, IL 61820.)

Joseph P. Kennedy, Jr., Foundation. *Let's play to grow.* Washington, DC: Author. (Available from Joseph P. Kennedy, Jr., Foundation, 1350 New York Avenue, NW, Suite 500, Washington, DC 20005.)

Lerner, J. (1981). *Learning disabilities: Theories, diagnosis, and teaching strategies.* Boston: Houghton Mifflin.

Leviton, D., & Santoro, L.C. (1980). *Health, physical education, recreation and dance for the older adult: A modular approach.* Reston, VA: American Alliance for Health, Physical Education, Recreation and Dance. (Available from AAHPERD, 1900 Association Drive, Reston, VA 22091.)

Paralyzed Veterans of America. *An introduction to spinal cord injury.* Washington, DC: Author. (Available from Paralyzed Veterans of America, 801 18th Street, NW, Washington, DC 20006.)

Physical activities for the mentally retarded: Ideas for instruction. (1968). Reston, VA: American Alliance for Health, Physical Education, and Recreation.

Special Olympics developmental sports skills program. Washington, DC: Special Olympics.

Appendix   **B**

Forms and Lists for Instructors

The following applications, forms, checklists, and activity sheets can help with aquatics programs. They are only representative samples; amend them as needed for any particular situation.

APPLICATION FOR ADMISSION
TO AQUATICS CLASS

Name of applicant _____

Age _____ Sex _____ Birth date _____

Name of parent or guardian _____

Home address _____

Home phone _____ Business or emergency phone _____

Is applicant attending school? _____

Name of school _____

Grade level _____

Has applicant ever been in water? ____ Pool ____ Beach ____

Does applicant swim? ____ To what extent? _____

_____ In deep water? _____

Disability:

_____ Physically disabled   _____ Mentally disabled

_____ Emotionally disturbed   _____ Socially disabled

_____ Other

Special problems or limitations _____

_____

Precautions to be observed _____

_____

Helpful suggestions/information to assist instructor in working
with student _____

_____

_____

_____

_____

_____

_____

_____

_____

_____

_____

Applicant has my permission to participate in aquatics programs.
_____ Yes _____ No

Restrictions _____

Name of physician _____

Address _____

I give my permission for medical treatment, if I cannot be
contacted. _____ Yes _____ No

I give my permission for an ambulance to be called in an
emergency. _____ Yes _____ No

I give my permission for the applicant to ride with volunteer
drivers on field trips or other activities connected with the
program. _____ Yes _____ No

Occasionally photographs of the swimming program are taken
for news stories. Please sign if we have your permission to take
pictures of the applicant. _____

Date _____

Parent or guardian's signature _____

PERMISSION SLIP

I give my permission for my child _____
to attend the _____ program. I accept full
responsibility for his or her physical condition and give my permission for program officials to call a doctor or other designated
person if I cannot be reached in the event of an emergency.

I will not hold the sponsoring organization liable for accident
or injury that might occur in this program.

Date _____ Signature _____

I permit my child's photograph to be taken in publicizing the
program. _____ Yes _____ No

MEDIC ALERT TAG

People with medical conditions should wear medic alert tags for easy identification in case of accident. Information can include the following:

Name _____

_____
Address   Telephone

In emergency notify:

Name _____

_____
Address   Telephone

Physician to be contacted:

Name _____

_____
Address   Telephone

Date of inoculations:

_____
Small Pox   Tetanus   Typhoid

_____
Measles   Polio (Salk or Sabin)

_____
Diptheria   Others

Conditions (e.g., diabetic, epileptic, or cardiac)

_____

_____

_____

Allergies (including medication)

_____

_____

Present medication

_____

_____

Other information

_____

_____

_____

_____

_____

A variety of medic alert tags are available commercially.

PROGRAM CHECKLIST

Name _____

Considerations   Program Dates

Medical:
   Epileptic   _____   A _____

   Medication _____   B _____

   Heart   _____   C _____

   Other   _____   D _____

                 _____

Toileting _____

Ambulation _____

Sections	A	B	C	D
Bus/van				
Locker room				
Enter/exit				
Survival				
Basic skills				

Comments

_____

_____

_____

_____

_____

_____

_____

Bus/Van Checklist   Name _____

	A	B	C	D
Approaches bus/van				
Grabs door handle				
Pushes thumb on button				
Pulls door open				
Pulls self in via armrest				
Steps into van				
Sits on floor, feet hanging				
Pulls feet into van				
Locates seat				
Sits in seat				
Remains seated while moving				
Stands when ride ends				
Opens van door from inside				
Steps out of van				
Sits on floor				
Hangs feet outside				
Stands on ground				

Comments

_____

_____

_____

_____

_____

Locker Room Checklist   Name _____

	A	B	C	D
Locates locker				
Opens locker				
Identifies empty locker				
Unties shoes				
Removes shoes				
Removes shirt				
Places shirt in locker				
Removes bra				
Removes pants				
Removes underwear				
Places all in locker				
Takes suit from container				
Puts feet through leg holes				
Rolls bottoms up				
Puts top on (if female)				
Fastens top				
Places bag/suitcase in front locker				
Closes locker tightly				
Enters shower area				
Turns shower on				
Showers				
Turns shower off				
Toilets				

Comments

_____

_____

_____

Enter/Exit Checklist　　Name _____

	A		B		C		D	
	Pre	Post	Pre	Post	Pre	Post	Pre	Post
Approaches ladder								
Places hands on rails								
Lowers self to sit using rails								
Puts feet into water								
Places feet onto step								
Lowers self into water								
Steps down to next step								
Lowers self to bottom								
Stands on bottom								
Releases rails								
Puts hands on side of pool								
Walks holding side of pool								
Takes instructor's hands								
Walks with instructor, two hands								
Walks with instructor, one hand								
Releases instructor's hands								
Stands in chest-deep water								
Walks in chest-deep water								
Approaches ladder								
Grasps ladder rails, two hands								
Steps up to foot on first step								
Pulls self up								
Steps to next step up								
Pulls self up								
Stands on deck between rails								

Comments

_____

_____

_____

Survival Checklist   Name _____

	A		B		C		D	
	Pre	Post	Pre	Post	Pre	Post	Pre	Post
Does not breathe or swallow water when face is submerged								
Expels water entering mouth during swimming								
Lifts face from water when submerged								
Holds instructor's hands while floating on stomach								
Holds pool edge while floating on stomach with instructor holding feet up								
Holds as above from back position								
Holds onto pool edge when feet are swept out from under								
Reaches/grabs for pool edge when allowed to drop from stomach floating position at arm's length								
As above except floats beside pool edge at arm's length								
Grabs for floating object extended by instructor when dropped from prone float by assistant								
Stands from previous objective								
Stands from drop from floating position on stomach								
Stands from drop from back floating position								

Comments

_____

_____

_____

Basic Skills Checklist   Name _____

	A		B		C		D	
	Pre	Post	Pre	Post	Pre	Post	Pre	Post
Jumps up and down								
Blows bubbles								
Puts face underwater								
Kicks feet								
Strokes arms								
Floats on stomach								
Floats on back								
Jumps into shallow water (waist deep)								
Prone glides								
Recovers footing from glide								
Breathes rhythmically								
Does human strokes								
Jumps into deep water								

Comments

_____

_____

_____

_____

PROGRESSION SHEET

Name _____

_____ 1. Adjusts to water.

_____ 2. Gets into pool properly.

_____ 3. Gets out of pool properly.

_____ 4. Sits on edge and kicks.

_____ 5. Walks across pool with help.

_____ 6. Walks across pool alone.

_____ 7. Walks across pool blowing bubbles.

_____ 8. Jumps like a bunny across pool.

_____ 9. Floats on front with help using flotation devices.

_____ 10. Floats on back with help using flotation devices.

_____ 11. Pulls on front while kicking using flotation devices.

_____ 12. Pulls on back while kicking using flotation devices.

_____ 13. Walks across pool with human armstroke.

_____ 14. Does paddle stroke with help using flotation devices.

_____ 15. Jumps in with help.

_____ 16. Jumps in five times alone.

_____ 17. Plays water games with others.

_____ 18. Kicks across with kickboard.

_____ 19. Uses fins.

_____ 20. Opens eyes under water.

Safety skills should be taught as soon as possible.

YMCA and American Red Cross certification is given when the participant is able to achieve skills required by these organizations.

SKILL SHEET 1

Name _____

_____ 1. Gets in the pool properly.

_____ 2. Gets out of the pool properly.

_____ 3. Blows bubbles well.

_____ 4. Walks across with no help.

_____ 5. Walks across with face in water.

_____ 6. Does human stroke kick with help to 10 counts.

_____ 7. Does flutter kick with help to 10 counts.

_____ 8. Opens eyes under water.

_____ 9. Does human armstroke with help.

_____ 10. Does crawl armstroke with help.

_____ 11. Bobs slowly five times.

_____ 12. Floats on back with help and recovers.

_____ 13. Jumps in with help.

_____ 14. Does front glide and recovers.

_____ 15. Jumps in five times alone.

_____ 16. Jumps in alone, getting head under.

_____ 17. Walks across with human armstroke and face in water.

_____ 18. Does waterbug float on front alone for five counts.

_____ 19. Bobs slowly 10 times.

_____ 20. Picks up object from bottom.

_____ 21. Does waterbug sitting dive.

_____ 22. Swims alone.

_____ 23. Does waterbug float on back alone for five counts.

_____ 24. Does flutter kick on back with help for 10 counts.

_____ 25. Does winging on the back alone for 10 counts.

_____ 26. Bobs with rhythmic breathing.

_____ 27. Does waterbug diving glide.

_____ 28. Swims five strokes alone in any combination.

_____ 29. Swims under water one body length.

_____ 30. Does cork float for five counts.

_____ 31. Does flutter back scull for 10 counts.

_____ 32. Swims across pool alone.

_____ 33. Rolls from front to back.

Flotation devices can be used to assist in developing skills and endurance as needed. Safety skill should be mastered.

YMCA and American Red Cross certification is given when the participant is able to achieve skills required by these organizations.

SKILL SHEET 2

Name _____

Skills must be executed in deep water unless otherwise indicated. From this skill sheet on, the emphasis should be on *endurance*.

_____ 1. Ducks down to bottom facing wall and comes back up.

_____ 2. Treads water for 1 minute using one of the following kicks: scissors, frog, flutter, or whip.

3. Does one of the following floats for 10 counts:

_____ Jellyfish float.

_____ Horizontal backfloat.

_____ Balanced backfloat.

_____ Vertical backfloat.

_____ 4. Does jumping surface dive in chest-deep water.

_____ 5. Jumps off diving board and swims to the side.

_____ 6. Jumps in, levels off, and swims 20 feet.

_____ 7. Changes position.

_____ 8. Changes direction.

_____ 9. Bobs 10 times with one breath between each bob.

_____ 10. Does standing dive, swims 20 feet, turns on top of water, and swims back (perfect form not required).

_____ 11. Does steamboat for width of pool.

_____ 12. Does backfloat and frog kick across pool.

_____ 13. Does elementary back armstroke across pool.

_____ 14. Does three porpoise dives across pool.

_____ 15. Does kneeling dive off board.

_____ 16. Jumps in, swims 20 feet, reverses direction, and returns on back.

_____ 17. Does standing front dive.

_____ 18. Does elementary backstroke for width of pool.

_____ 19. Does flutter back scull for width of pool.

_____ 20. Plunges, dives under water, and swims 15 feet.

_____ 21. Ducks down to bottom, swims under water across pool.

_____ 22. Does frontcrawl with rhythmic breathing across pool.

_____ 23. Survival swims for 1 minute.

The kick on the elementary survival swim or breaststroke should be adapted to the ability of the disability. Safety skills should be reviewed. Flotation devices can be used to assist in developing skills and endurance as needed.

YMCA and American Red Cross certification is given when the participant is able to achieve skills according to the requirements set by these organizations.

SKILL SHEET 3

Name _____

_____ 1. Changes position (front to back).

_____ 2. Changes position (back to front).

_____ 3. Practices assisting with pole and wading human chain.

_____ 4. Does flutter kick on front across pool.

_____ 5. Does flutter kick on back across pool.

_____ 6. Does sidestroke (arms and legs) across pool.

_____ 7. Does breaststroke (arms and legs) across pool.

_____ 8. Uses ring buoy (throwing, heaving line) to tow someone using kickboard.

_____ 9. Does elementary backstroke across pool.

_____ 10. Does backfloat in deep water (1 minute).

_____ 11. Does scull on back (hands at side) across pool.

_____ 12. Does feet-first scull across pool.

_____ 13. Stays afloat in one spot for 30 seconds.

_____ 14. Does overarm sidestroke (two times to rope and back).

_____ 15. Treads water, does scissors kick for 1 minute.

_____ 16. Swims underwater across pool.

_____ 17. Makes a running jump from low elevation (enters with feet together).

_____ 18. Does standing front dive from board.

_____ 19. Swims in place/treads water for 5 minutes, not touching sides or bottom.

_____ 20. Swims two pool lengths using no more than two different strokes.

Optional special skills include simple synchronized swimming, survival swimming, use of a life jacket, and doing a lifesaving jump. Flotation devices can be used to assist in developing skills and endurance as needed.

YMCA and American Red Cross certification is given when the participant is able to achieve skills according to the requirements set by these organizations.

SKILL SHEET 4

Name _____

_____ 1. Does sidestroke for 60 yards with proper turns.

_____ 2. Does elementary backstroke for 60 yards.

_____ 3. Does crawl stroke for 60 yards with proper turns.

_____ 4. Does backcrawl for 20 yards.

_____ 5. On back, legs only, does inverted scissors or breast kick for 40 yards.

_____ 6. Corkscrew swims to the rope.

_____ 7. Torpedo swims across pool.

_____ 8. Does jackknife (pike) surface dive into 8-foot water and swims three body lengths.

_____ 9. Does tuck surface dive into 8-foot water and swims three body lengths.

_____ 10. Does feet-first surface dive into 8-foot water and swims three body lengths.

_____ 11. Does long shallow dive (racing or starting dive).

_____ 12. Does feet-first entry into deep water (feet together).

_____ 13. Jumps from low board.

_____ 14. Does standing dive from low board.

_____ 15. Does back dive from low board.

_____ 16. Swims six lengths, using two strokes.

_____ 17. Dives in, gliding or swimming under water to rope.

_____ 18. Treads water for 5 minutes.

_____ 19. Swims with clothes on, disrobing and using clothes for support.

_____ 20. Practices with life jacket.

_____ 21. Does lifesaving jump.

_____ 22. Swims in a line and in a circle.

_____ 23. Does wrist tow and extension tow.

Flotation devices can be used to assist in developing skills and endurance as needed.

YMCA and American Red Cross certification is given when the participant is able to achieve skills according to the requirements set by these organizations.

Appendix C

Commercial Outlets for Adaptive Equipment

Aquanaids
Wm. M. Smith Associations
50 Dynamic Drive, Unit 3
Scarborough, Ontario MIV2W2
(416) 293-8200

Bubbles—Flotation Devices
J and B Foam Fabricators
PO Box 144
Ludington, MI 49431
(616) 843-2448

Danmar Products, Inc.
2390 Winewood
Ann Arbor, MI 48103
(313) 761-1990

Flotation Devices
251 Allen
West Chicago, IL 60185
(312) 293-1797

Personal Flotation Devices
The Flaghouse
18 West 18th Street
New York, NY 10011

Pool Lift
J.E. Nolan & Company, Inc.
PO Box 43201
Louisville, KY 40243
(502) 425-0883

Ramps, Stairs, Steps
AFW Company of North America
Exchange National Bank Building
North Union Street
Olean, NY 14760
(716) 372-2935

Samarite Hospital Supplies
PO Box 2490
Holyoke, MA 01041
(413) 536-3321

Ted Hoyer and Company, Inc.
2222 Minnesota Street
PO Box 2744
Oshkosh, WI 54903
(414) 231-7970

Trans Aid Corporation
1609 East Del Amo
Carson, CA 97046
(213) 538-8966

Transfer Tier Steps
Triad Technology, Inc.
6005 Galster Road
East Syracuse, NY 13057
(315) 437-4089

Glossary

Abduction: A movement away from the midline of the body.

Adduction: A movement toward the midline of the body.

Allergy: A hypersensitivity to a specific substance, such as food, pollen, dust, insect bites, drugs, or chemicals, or to an atmospheric condition, such as heat, cold, or pollution, which in moderate amounts is harmless to most people.

Alzheimer's: A disease that is the major cause of senile dementia. First the mind deteriorates, with its core of essential recent and long-past memories; then the body dies. Those with Alzheimer's disease may be unable to walk or control bodily functions. Gradually the person sinks into a coma and never regains consciousness.

Ambulation Aids and Prosthetics: Devices, such as crutches or artificial legs, used to assist diabled people in moving.

Amputees: People with one or more limbs missing. The limbs may have been missing at birth or have been lost because of accident or surgery.

Anterior: Toward the front or ventral side of the body.

Aphasia: A total or partial loss of the ability to use or understand words, usually caused by brain illness or injury.

Arthritis: An inflammation of a joint or joints. The term covers nearly 100 conditions that cause aching and pain in the joints and connective tissues throughout the body.

Asthma: An allergic response characterized by such symptoms as shortness of breath, tightness in the chest, and wheezing. If untreated, it can lead to respiratory paralysis and possible death.

Ataxia: Lack of balance and coordination.

Autism: The inability to respond appropriately to external stimuli, such as sounds and commands, or the complete inability to respond. The autistic person may appear to be deaf and mute. Autism may be congenital or may follow severe traumatic incidents.

Barrier Free: Accessible for all people.

BEH: Bureau of Education for the Handicapped; now OSERS (Office of Special Education and Rehabilitative Services, U.S. Department of Education).

Bilateral: Pertaining to both sides of the body.

Blind: Sightless or with severely limited vision.

Brain Damage: Impairment to the thought processes due to accident or disease.

Brittle Bones: Also known as osteogenesis imperfecta. This is caused by demineralization of the bones and is characterized by bone fragility.

Cancer: A malignant growth anywhere in the body. It can be solid, such as a tumor in the brain or the breast, or it can be a disorderly growth of tissue cells anywhere in the body, such as in the bloodstream, lymph nodes, or bone marrow. If the process continues unchecked, the normal structure and function of an organ will be destroyed.

Cardiac: Conditions and diseases related to the heart.

Catheter: Artificial tube inserted in the bladder for urinary drainage, usually attached to a leg bag that requires periodic emptying.

Cerebral Palsy: A brain-centered disorder affecting muscular control and sensory functions.

Cerebrovascular Accident: Strokes and apoplexy; a hemorrhage or a clot in a blood vessel within the brain. Coma, loss of speech, partial paralysis, and loss of functions normal to the affected portion of the brain often result.

Circuit Training: Station-to-station training. By setting up various activities in different areas of a pool, gymnasium, or classroom, students can learn a variety of skills, going from one to another progressively. Circuit training enables a student to progress at an individual pace from one station to another at his or her own level of fitness and skill.

Circumduction: A circular movement of a limb.

Colostomy: Incision of an artificial opening into the colon for drainage of wastes.

Concussion: A condition of impaired functioning of the brain as the result of a violent blow or impact.

Congenital: A problem resulting from heredity or the prenatal environment.

Contracture: A shortening of muscles, tendons, or fibrous tissues around a joint that may be caused by spasticity, disuse, or maintaining one position for prolonged periods of time.

CVA: A cerebrovascular accident.

Cyanosis: A bluish coloration of the skin caused by lack of oxygen in the blood. This may be the result of submersion in cold water.

Deaf: Totally or partially unable to hear. Deafness may be congenital, it may result from illness or injury, or it may be part of the normal process of aging.

Developmental Disabilities: Physical and/or mental disabilities that originate before age 21, continue indefinitely, and constitute a significant problem.

Diabetes: A metabolic disturbance in which the pancreas cannot produce a sufficient amount of the hormone insulin necessary to use and properly store sugar.

Diplegia: A partial or complete paralysis of both upper or both lower limbs.

Disability: An impairment or impairments that limit the execution of some skills or performance of some activities.

Distal: Farthest from the center or point of attachment or origin; farthest away from the trunk of the body.

Dorsal: Toward the back side.

Dyslexia: The inability to interpret written language. An individual with this condition can see normally but has difficulty interpreting what is being seen and therefore has problems reading and writing.

Epilepsy/Seizure Disorder: Any convulsive disorder. It can occur by itself or in conjunction with other conditions.

Epileptic Seizure: A state produced by an excessive neuronal discharge within the central nervous system; a convulsion.

Eversion: The process of turning outward or inside out.

Extension: The process of straightening a flexed part.

Extensors: Muscles that straighten a joint.

External Rotation: Rotation away from the body.

Flaccid: With little or no muscle tone; extremity appears floppy with little if any voluntary or involuntary movement.

Flexion: The process of bending.

Gait: Manner, pattern, or style of walking.

Habilitation: Maintaining or improving a person's skill level through treatment and training.

Handicapped: A person with a disadvantage or hindrance. Disabled is the preferred word to use.

Head Injury: Injury to the head resulting in impairment to the thought processes; brain damage.

Hearing Impaired: Having any hearing problem that interferes with learning.

Hemiparesis: Weakness on one side of the body.

Hemiplegia: A motor and sensory paralysis of one side or one half of the body.

Hemophilia: A disorder of the blood coagulating mechanism that leads to easy bruising and extensive hemorrhages involving the muscular and subcutaneous tissues of joints or any organ of the body.

Hydrocephalus: An excess of cerebrospinal fluid within the brain structure. The obstruction of adequate spinal fluid drainage results in destruction of brain tissue.

Hyperextension: Extreme or excessive extension of a limb or part.

Hypertension: High blood pressure.

Hypothermia: Generalized lowering of body temperature. Various disabilities cause different responses to cold.

IEP: Individual Education Plan, as required by Public Law 94-142. This is a written statement of the instructional plan for a handicapped child, which is tailored to the child's specific needs and abilities.

IHP: Individual Habilitative Plan. This is a plan of care created to develop skills that will maintain the abilities of the disabled individual. Such a plan is most often developed by county and state agencies in cooperation with residential facilities.

Impaired: Having an identifiable organic or functional condition, with some part of the body missing or one or more parts of the body not functioning adequately.

Incontinence: Loss of bowel and/or bladder control.

Inferior: Under or lower.

Interval Training: Teaching various skills slowly and in intervals, going back to those with which the student is having difficulty rather than concentrating on a skill until it is mastered. The student performs a series of activities at his or her own level or pace for a specified length of time.

Inversion: The process of turning in.

IPP: Individual Program Plan. This is a program plan developed to fit the particular needs of an individual or a group of individuals with similar abilities. An IPP for a group would include all the skills and activities to be taught and evaluated.

Lateral: Away from the midline.

Lateral Flexion: Bending to the side.

Learning Disabilities: Learning problems arising from perceptual, conceptual, or subtle coordination problems. These difficulties may be accompanied by behavior problems in children with potentially average, average, or above average intelligence.

Leukemia: A disease of blood-forming organs, characterized by excessively large numbers of white blood cells in the bloodstream; cancer of the blood.

Mainstream: Integration of disabled people into programs for the nondisabled.

Mastectomy: Removal of a breast that has a malignant tumor.

Medial: Near or toward the midline of the body.

Mental Illness: A wide range of illnesses ranging from the mental and emotional problems of young people, which may manifest themselves through learning disabilities, "acting out" behavior, delusions, hallucinations, or inability to socially adjust, to the problems of the adult who is totally withdrawn, antisocial, or otherwise unable to function in society.

Mental Retardation: Impaired or incomplete mental development or function attributable to a variety of causes. For example, cretinism is a malfunction of the thyroid gland, Down's syndrome is a chromosomal abnormality, and phenylketonuria (PKU) is a metabolic disturbance in which the body cannot convert phenylalanine to protein.

Midline: An imaginary line drawn through the middle of the body from the superior to the inferior point.

Monoplegia: Paralysis of a single limb or body part.

Multiple Sclerosis: A disease of the central nervous system chiefly affecting the white matter of the brain and spinal cord. It is "multiple" both chronologically and anatomically: It is characterized by relapses followed by periods of partial and sometimes complete recovery, and it affects many parts of the nervous system.

Muscle Re-Education: Bringing a muscle into active use through a series of planned activities.

Muscle Substitution: Employing a different muscle or muscle group to replace a muscle that can no longer be used.

Muscle Tone: Degree of tension in muscle when muscle is at rest.

Muscular Dystrophy: A chronic disease of the muscles with gradual weakening over time. The muscles waste, and weakening become progressively worse until the person is confined to a wheelchair and eventually to bed.

Neurological: Pertaining to diseases of the nervous system. Both mental and physical conditions may be present. Some neurological diseases are cerebral palsy, Parkinson's disease, and multiple sclerosis.

Neuromuscular: Pertaining to the nerves and muscles.

Opposition: Bringing the thumb to meet the fingertips.

Orthopedically Impaired: Having impairments including the congenital, such as dislocated arms and hips, spina bifida, club feet, scoliosis, and other malformations; the traumatic, such as paraplegia, amputations, and peripheral nerve injury; and infections, such as osteomyelitis, poliomyelitis, tuberculosis of the bone, and nerve degeneration.

Osers: Acronym for Office of Special Education and Rehabilitative Services, U.S. Department of Education.

Osteoporosis: A condition found primarily in older, thin, white women in which the bone mass slowly is reabsorbed by the body leaving the bone that remains fragile and susceptible to fracture.

Paraplegia: Motor and sensory paralysis of the lower half of the body, usually caused by injury or disease of the spinal column.

Parkinson's Disease: A chronic, progressive central nervous system disorder characterized by slowness, lack of purposeful movement, muscular rigidity, and tremors.

Perthes Disease: Demineralization of the bone characterized by deformity and abnormal growth of the hipbone, precluding weight bearing on one or both lower extremities.

Posterior: Toward the back or dorsal side of the body.

Prescription Teaching: Education for an individual that takes into account medical, rehabilitative, and other factors. The teaching plan often is devised by a team, including physician and health caregivers, therapists, social workers, parents, and the student.

Pronation: Turning the hand downward.

Prone: Lying in a face-down position.

Proximal: Closer to the trunk of the body.

Public Law 94-142: Federal law mandating and regulating public education of disabled children 3 to 21 years of age.

Quad Cane: Cane with a four-pronged base to provide greater stability.

Quadriplegia: Partial or complete paralysis of all four limbs.

Range of Motion (ROM): How far a joint can be moved voluntarily through active motion by an individual. There is also active assistive motion, with assistance by another person; and passive motion, with assistance, initiation, and follow-through by another individual or with a healthy part of the person's body.

Regression: A movement backward to an earlier stage of mental or physical development, often associated with mental illness and the inability to adjust to the present situation.

Rehabilitation: Restoring health and efficiency through treatment and training.

Rotation: Recurrent turning of body part.

Rubella Syndrome: Impairments caused when a woman contracts rubella (German measles) during the first 3 months of pregnancy. Mental retardation, blindness, deafness, cataracts, heart disease, and microcephalis as well as multiple impairments have been associated with first-trimester rubella.

Spastic: Increased muscle tone, manifested most commonly in the extremities, that may appear drawn in toward the body and flexed. The extremity resists movement and may demonstrate involuntary motions or spasms if moved abruptly.

Special Education: Public school instruction designed to meet the unique needs of a developmentally disabled child.

Spina Bifida: A congenital defect of the spinal column, usually involving improper closure of the vertebral column. Although the lives of children born with this condition usually can be saved by surgery, many such youngsters have considerable physical and intellectual disabilities.

Spinal and Postural Deviations: Distortions of the backbone and posture. The most common are caused by polio, which leaves some muscles too weak to balance the pull of the remaining, stronger muscles; bad posture, both while in motion and while standing still; and other conditions that leave muscles on one side of the spine stronger than muscles on the opposite side.

Spinal Cord Lesions: Complete or partial loss of sensations and reflexes after a spinal injury.

Station-to-Station Teaching: Teaching that involves setting up various activities in different parts (stations) of the pool, gymnasium, or classroom. Students progress from one station to another and may stay at a station for a specific length of time, go back and forth between stations, or visit favorite activities.

Stroke: A blood vessel accident within the skull. The term may describe symptoms caused by rupture of a blood vessel that supplies blood to some part of the brain; a clot or thrombosis in a blood vessel within the brain; or a blood clot that has broken away from some distant point, usually the inner lining of the left side of the heart, and traveled to the brain, where it clogs an artery. Functions normal to the affected area of the brain may be impaired. Coma, loss of speech, or paralysis on one side of the body may ensue.

Substance Abuse: Overindulgence in prescribed medication, over-the-counter drugs, street drugs, or alcohol.

Superior: Upper or higher.

Supination: Process of turning palms up.

Supine: Lying in a face-up position.

Therapeutic Recreation: Leisure time activities structured to be of assistance in the physical, intellectual, emotional, and social rehabilitative process.

Therapy: Therapy is the treatment of illness or disability. Some types of therapy include occupational therapy, physical therapy, recreation therapy, music therapy, play therapy, swimming therapy, and speech therapy. These are therapy modules for which training and certification are available. Therapy may refer to any specific intervention modality that will improve the ability of the individual to learn, work, or enjoy recreation.

Triplegia: Partial or complete paralysis affecting three limbs.

Visually Impaired: Being incapable of carrying out specific visual tasks because of impairments of one or more of the functions of sight.

Voluntary Muscles: Muscles under the control of the will.